MooTools 1.3 Cookbook

Over 110 highly effective recipes to turbo-charge the user interface of any web-enabled Internet application and web page

Jay Larry G. Johnston

BIRMINGHAM - MUMBAI

MooTools 1.3 Cookbook

First published: July 2011

Production Reference: 1150711

Published by Packt Publishing Ltd.
32 Lincoln Road
Olton
Birmingham, B27 6PA, UK.

ISBN 978-1-849515-68-9

www.packtpub.com

Cover Image by Parag Kadam (paragvkadam@gmail.com)

Credits

Author
Jay Larry G. Johnston

Reviewers
Harald Kirschner
Andy Meerwaldt
Thiago Santos

Acquisition Editor
Sarah Cullington

Development Editors
Hyacintha D'Souza
Kartikey Pandey

Technical Editors
Conrad Sardinha
Aaron Rosario

Project Coordinator
Michelle Quadros

Proofreader
Chris Smith

Indexer
Hemangini Bari

Production Coordinator
Shantanu Zagade

Cover Work
Shantanu Zagade

About the Author

Jay's first web work was in 1996 for the United States Army where he served the 5/5 Battalion Headquarters with the 2nd Infantry Division in South Korea.

Currently full time as Senior PHP Developer for ICGLink, Inc. managing high-end, custom development for the 2,000+ client base, Jay holds certifications in Linux, MySQL, and PHP5.

Introduced to the MooTools framework in 2007 while on permanent contract at Marshall Space Flight Center, Jay has incorporated Moo into every single new development since and frequently writes canned moo-solutions for use within the company.

To know more about the author, visit his website at `http://jayjohnston.com`.

About the Reviewer

Andy Meerwaldt is a Dutch web developer with a BIT (Bachelor of Information Technology) degree, and has been developing PHP applications since 2004. He started using the Kohana Framework as his default framework. He has improved on his skill in Object Oriented Programming and the use of Design patterns over time. His aim is to build better and smoother web applications with full functionality for raising the user experience.

Besides PHP Andy is experienced in JavaScript and is still adopting new techniques and best practices for getting the most out of the Web. Further on, he's interested in high scalability, performance, and usability.

www.PacktPub.com

Support files, eBooks, discount offers and more

You might want to visit www.PacktPub.com for support files and downloads related to your book.

Did you know that Packt offers eBook versions of every book published, with PDF and ePub files available? You can upgrade to the eBook version at www.PacktPub.com and, as a print book customer, you are entitled to a discount on the eBook copy. Get in touch with us at service@packtpub.com for more details.

At www.PacktPub.com, you can also read a collection of free technical articles, sign up for a range of free newsletters, and receive exclusive discounts and offers on Packt books and eBooks.

http://PacktLib.PacktPub.com

Do you need instant solutions to your IT questions? PacktLib is Packt's online digital book library. Here, you can access, read, and search across Packt's entire library of books.

Why subscribe?

- ▶ Fully searchable across every book published by Packt
- ▶ Copy and paste, print, and bookmark content
- ▶ On demand and accessible via web browser

Free access for Packt account holders

If you have an account with Packt at www.PacktPub.com, you can use this to access PacktLib today and view nine entirely free books. Simply use your login credentials for immediate access.

Bright Holly, Christian Lake, and Kwon Myoung-hee, thank you, my dear ones.

Table of Contents

Preface

MooTools is a JavaScript framework that abstracts the JavaScript language. JavaScript itself, complex in syntax, provides the tools to write a layer of content interaction for each different browser. MooTools abstracts those individual, browser-specific layers to allow cross-browser scripting in an easy-to-read and easy-to-remember syntax.

Animation and interaction, once the domain of Flash, are being taken by storm by the MooTools JavaScript framework, which can cause size, shape, color, and opacity to transition smoothly. Discover how to use Ajax to bring data to today's web page users who demand interactivity without clunky page refreshes. When searching for animation and interactivity solutions that work, *MooTools 1.3 Cookbook* has individual, reusable code examples that get you running fast!

MooTools 1.3 Cookbook readies programmers to animate, perform Ajax, and attach event listeners in a simple format where each section provides a clear and cross-browser compatible sketch of how to solve a problem, whether reading from the beginning to the end or browsing directly to a particular recipe solution.

MooTools 1.3 Cookbook provides instant solutions to MooTools problems—whatever you want to do with MooTools, this book will tell you how to do it.

MooTools 1.3 Cookbook is presented in a progressive order that builds concepts and ideas, while simultaneously being a collection of powerful individual, stand-alone, recipe solutions.

What this book covers

Chapter 1, Oldies-but-Goodies: Foundational Moo. Learn foundational MooTool basics like including MooTools in HTML, making and looping over arrays, grabbing elements, and dragging items!

Chapter 2, Switching Paddles Midstream: Changing HTML After Page Load. Delve into changing HTML after load with working examples of finding, moving, adding, and removing elements and groups of elements.

Chapter 3, And on the 8th Day: Creating HTML Elements. Create HTML elements like IFRAMEs, A tags, and form elements and inject them into tables, table rows, and DIV elements.

Chapter 4, That's Not All Folks: Animation and Scrolling. Animate the Internet with morphs, tweens, slides, and scrolls. Make thumbnails scroll and users drool.

Chapter 5, Mr. Clean Uses Ajax: Remote Asynchronous Calls. Fire remote Ajax calls, on page, bringing them into the Web 2.0 arena where user interfaces are cool and fun.

Chapter 6, Easy Come, Easy Go: Drag and Drop. Drag and drop your way to shopping carts and interfaces that create return users and Internet buzz.

Chapter 7, Knock and the Door Will Open: Events and Listeners. Open the door to flexibility and functionality by adding event listeners and chains of actions.

Chapter 8, Dynamite! (Movin' On Up): Working with Transitions. Use transitions to save space, welcome users, make ducks bounce, and golf balls roll.

Chapter 9, WTFudge is Going On?: Troubleshooting MooTools. Troubleshoot scripting issues with tools of the professional development trade.

Chapter 10, Enough Is Never Enough: Extending MooTools. MooTools is highly extensible and allows for simple extension of existing classes and DOM elements. Level up by extending MooTools with custom plugins.

What you need for this book

To run the examples in the book following software will be required:

- Web Server: Apache recommended

    - Apache 1.3 or Apache 2.x, Apache 2.x recommended
    - Microsoft IIS 5, IIS 6 or IIS 7, IIS 7 recommended

#	Software Name	URL
1	Apache	`http://httpd.apache.org/`
2	Microsoft IIS	`http://www.iis.net/`

Additionally the following tools are helpful, but are not strictly required:

- PHP:

    - PHP 5.2 recommended
    - PHP 5.2 or PHP 5.3, PHP 5.2 recommended

▶   ColdFusion:

    ▶   ColdFusion 8 or 9 recommended

#	Software Name	URL
1	PHP	`http://php.net`
2	ColdFusion	`http://adobe.com/support/coldfusion/downloads.html`

Who this book is for

Users of all skill levels will find this book useful. Advanced users will expand their knowledge of MooTools interaction. Intermediate users will delve into new concepts of usage. Novice users will find they are carefully taken through each facet of knowledge necessary to rapidly become intermediate users.

Conventions

In this book, you will find a number of styles of text that distinguish between different kinds of information. Here are some examples of these styles, and an explanation of their meaning.

Code words in text are shown as follows: "Please do always include a DOCTYPE, and opening HTML, HEAD, TITLE, and META tag for the HTTP-EQUIV and CONTENT".

A block of code is set as follows:

```
$('my_trigger').addEvent('click',function()  {
    this.set('html','Click  Me<br/>'+(++count));
...
```

When we wish to draw your attention to a particular part of a code block, the relevant lines or items are set in bold:

```
<div id="my_trigger"
  style="width:100px; height:100px;
  border:1px solid #BEBEBE;
  line-height:50px; text-align:center;">You Found Me!</div>
<noscript>JavaScript is disabled.</noscript>
```

New terms and **important words** are shown in bold. Words that you see on the screen, in menus or dialog boxes for example, appear in the text like this: "The link labeled **GET MOO.FX FOR MOOTOOLS** leads us to MooTools".

[Warnings or important notes appear in a box like this.]

[Tips and tricks appear like this.]

Reader feedback

Feedback from our readers is always welcome. Let us know what you think about this book—what you liked or may have disliked. Reader feedback is important for us to develop titles that you really get the most out of.

To send us general feedback, simply send an e-mail to feedback@packtpub.com, and mention the book title via the subject of your message.

If there is a book that you need and would like to see us publish, please send us a note in the **SUGGEST A TITLE** form on www.packtpub.com or e-mail suggest@packtpub.com.

If there is a topic that you have expertise in and you are interested in either writing or contributing to a book, see our author guide on www.packtpub.com/authors.

Customer support

Now that you are the proud owner of a Packt book, we have a number of things to help you to get the most from your purchase.

Downloading the example code

You can download the example code files for all Packt books you have purchased from your account at http://www.PacktPub.com. If you purchased this book elsewhere, you can visit http://www.PacktPub.com/support and register to have the files e-mailed directly to you.

Errata

Although we have taken every care to ensure the accuracy of our content, mistakes do happen. If you find a mistake in one of our books—maybe a mistake in the text or the code—we would be grateful if you would report this to us. By doing so, you can save other readers from frustration and help us improve subsequent versions of this book. If you find any errata, please report them by visiting http://www.packtpub.com/support, selecting your book, clicking on the **errata submission form** link, and entering the details of your errata. Once your errata are verified, your submission will be accepted and the errata will be uploaded on our website, or added to any list of existing errata, under the Errata section of that title. Any existing errata can be viewed by selecting your title from http://www.packtpub.com/support.

Piracy

Piracy of copyright material on the Internet is an ongoing problem across all media. At Packt, we take the protection of our copyright and licenses very seriously. If you come across any illegal copies of our works, in any form, on the Internet, please provide us with the location address or website name immediately so that we can pursue a remedy.

Please contact us at copyright@packtpub.com with a link to the suspected pirated material.

We appreciate your help in protecting our authors, and our ability to bring you valuable content.

Questions

You can contact us at questions@packtpub.com if you are having a problem with any aspect of the book, and we will do our best to address it.

1
Oldies-but-Goodies: Foundational Moo

Foundational MooTool basics top the record charts both in the good old days and in this chapter: MooTool versions, documentation, and hosting:

- ▶ Elements, arrays, and objects
- ▶ Flat craziness like anonymous functions and arrays!

MooTroduction

All Packt Publishing Cookbook Series books are meant to be read without procedural constraint. That means, we can open any page in the book and just start *mooing*. This book, being a cookbook, follows that crucial precept while also harboring a secret agenda to move from smaller concepts to larger concepts for the benefit of any potentially existing procedural readers. Those of us that may be new to these concepts will benefit greatly from this chapter.

MooTools was conceived by Valerio Proietti and copy written under MIT License in 2006. We send a great round of roaring applause to Valerio for creating the Moo.FX (My Object Oriented Effects) plugin for Prototype, a JavaScript abstraction library. That work gave life to an arguably more effects-oriented (and highly extensible) abstraction layer of its own: MooTools (My Object Oriented Tools).

See also

Find more information about Moo.FX at `http://moofx.mad4milk.net/`. The link labeled **GET MOO.FX FOR MOOTOOLS** leads us to MooTools, which is exactly what we are delving into; so we continue, confident that with MooTools, we are getting what Moo.FX has become.

Knowing our MooTools version

This recipe is an introduction to the different MooTools versions and how to be sure we are coding in the right version.

Getting ready

[Not all are equal nor are backwards compatible!]

The biggest switch in compatibility came between MooTools 1.1 and MooTools 1.2. This *minor* version change caused clamor in the community given the rather *major* changes included. In our experience, we find that **1.2 and 1.3 MooTool scripts play well together** while 1.0 and 1.1 scripts tend to be agreeable as well. However, Moo's popularity spiked with version 1.1, and well-used scripts written with 1.0, like MooTabs, were upgraded to 1.1 when released. The exact note in Google Libraries for the version difference between 1.1 and 1.2 reads:

> Since 1.1 versions are not compatible with 1.2 versions, specifying version "1" will map to the latest 1.1 version (currently 1.1.2).

MooTools 1.1.1 has inline comments, which cause the uncompressed version to be about 180% larger than version 1.2.5 and 130% larger than the 1.3.0 release. When compressed, with YUI compression, 1.1 and 1.2 weigh in at about 65K while 1.3.0 with the CSS3 selectors is a modest 85K. In the code snippets, the compressed versions are denoted with a `c.js` file ending.

Two great additions in 1.3.0 that account for most of the difference in size from 1.2.5 are `Slick.Parser` and `Slick.Finder`. We may not need CSS3 parsing; so we may download the MooTools Core with only the particular class or classes we need. Browse `http://mootools.net/core/` and pick and choose the classes needed for the project. We should note that the best practice is to download all modules during development and pare down to what is needed when taking an application into production.

When we are more concerned with functionality than we are with performance and have routines that require backwards compatibility with MooTools 1.1, we can download the 1.2.5 version *with* the 1.1 classes from the MooTools download page at `http://mootools.net/download`. The latest MooTools version as of authoring is 1.3.0. All scripts within this cookbook are built and tested using MooTools version 1.3.0 as hosted by Google Libraries (more to follow on that in *this* chapter).

How to do it...

This is the basic HTML framework within which all recipes of this book will be launched and comprises the first recipe of the book:

```
<!DOCTYPE  html  PUBLIC  "-//W3C//DTD  XHTML  1.0  Transitional//EN"
  "http://www.w3.org/TR/xhtml1/DTD/xhtml1-transitional.dtd">
<html  xmlns="http://www.w3.org/1999/xhtml">
<head>
<title>MooTools Recipes</title>
    <meta http-equiv="content-type" content="text/html;charset=utf-8"
/>
```

 Note that the portion above is necessary but is not included in the other recipes to save space. Please do always include a DOCTYPE, and opening HTML, HEAD, TITLE, and META tag for the HTTP-EQUIV and CONTENT.

```
<script type="text/javascript" src="mootools-1.3.0.js"></script>

</head>
<body>
    <noscript>Your  Browser  has  JavaScript  Disabled.
    Please  use  industry  best  practices  for  coding
    in  JavaScript;  letting  users  know  they  are  missing
    out  is  crucial!</noscript>
    <script type="text/javascript">
    // best practice:  ALWAYS include a NOSCRIPT tag!

        var  mooversion  =  MooTools.version;

        var  msg  =  'version:  '+mooversion;
        document.write(msg);
        //  just  for  fun:
        var  question  =  'Use  MooTools  version
          '+msg+'?';
        var  yes  =  'It  is  as  you  have  requested!';
        var  no  =  "Please  change  the  mootools  source  attribute
          in  HTML->head->script.";
        //  give  'em  ham
        alert((confirm(question)?yes:no));
    </script>
</body>
</html>
```

How it works...

Inclusion of external libraries like MooTools is usually handled within the HEAD element of the HTML document. The NOSCRIPT tag will only be read by browsers that have their JavaScript disabled. The SCRIPT tag may be placed directly within the layout of the page.

There's more...

Using the XHTML doctype (or any doctype for that matter) allows your HTML to validate, helps browsers parse your pages faster, and helps the **Dynamic Object Model** (**DOM**) behave consistently. When our HTML does not validate, our JavaScript errors will be more random and difficult to solve.

Many seasoned developers have settled upon a favorite doctype. This allows them to become familiar with the ad-nauseam of cross browser oddities associated with that particular doctype. To further delve into doctypes, quirksmode, and other HTML specification esoterica, the heavily trafficked `http://www.quirksmode.org/css/quirksmode.html` provides an easy-to-follow and complete discourse.

See also

Be sure we are familiar with how non-sighted users browse our pages. We can make others' lives very difficult in the same stroke that we as programmers call *user friendly*. Check out the American Disabilities Act, ADA website for more information.

Finding MooTools documentation both new and old

Browsing `http://mootools.net/docs/core` will afford us the opportunity to use the version of our choice. The 1.2/1.3 demonstrations at the time of writing are expanding nicely. Tabs in the demonstrations at `http://mootools.net/demos` display each of the important elements of the demonstration.

MooTools had a major split at the minor revision number of 1.1. If working on a legacy project that still implements the deprecated MooTools version 1.1, take a shortcut to `http://docs111.mootools.net`.

Copying the demonstrations line-for-line, without studying them to see how they work, may afford our project the opportunity to become malicious code.

Using Google Library's MooTools scripts

Let Google maintain the core files and provide the bandwidth to serve them.

Getting ready

Google is leading the way in helping MooTools developers save time in the arenas of development, maintenance, and hosting by working together with the MooTools developers to host and deliver compressed and uncompressed versions of MooTools to our website visitors. Hosting on their servers eliminates the resources required to host, bandwidth required to deliver, and developer time required to maintain the requested, fully patched, and up-to-date version.

Usually we link to a minor version of a library to prevent major version changes that could cause unexpected behavior in our production code.

Google API keys that are required in the documentation to use Google Library can be easily and quickly obtained at: `http://code.google.com/apis/libraries/devguide.html#sign_up_for_an_api_key`.

How to do it...

Once you have the API Key, use the **script tag** method to include MooTools. For more information on loading the JavaScript API see `http://code.google.com/apis/ libraries/devguide.html#load_the_javascript_api_and_ajax_search_module`.

```
<!--script  type="text/javascript"  src="mootools-1.3.0.js">
</script-->
 <!--we've  got  ours  commented  out  so  that  we  can  use
      google's  here:-->

 <script  src="https://www.google.com/jsapi?key=OUR-KEY-HERE"
          type="text/javascript"></script>
 // the full src path is truncated for display here
 <script src="https://ajax.googleapis.com/.../mootools-yui-compressed.js"
          type="text/javascript"></script>
</head>
<body>
 <noscript>JavaScript  is  disabled.</noscript>
 <script type="text/javascript">
    var mooversion = MooTools.version;
    var msg = 'MooTools version: '+mooversion+' from Google';
    // show the msg in two different ways (just because)
    document.write(msg);
    alert(msg);
 </script>
```

Using `google.load()`, which is available to us when we include the Google Library API, we can make the inclusion code a bit more readable. See the line below that includes the string `jsapi?key=`. We replace `OUR-KEY-HERE` with our API key, which is tied to our domain name so Google can contact us if they detect a problem:

```
<!--script  type="text/javascript"  src="mootools-1.3.0.js"></script-
->
  <!--we've  got  ours  commented  out  so  that  we  can  use
google's
      here:-->
  <script  src="https://www.google.com/jsapi?key=OUR-KEY-HERE"
          type="text/javascript"></script>
  <script type="text/javascript">

  google.load("mootools", "1.2.5");

  </script>
</head>
```

```
<body>
  <noscript>JavaScript  is  disabled.</noscript>
  <script type="text/javascript">
    var mooversion = MooTools.version;
    var msg = 'MooTools version: '+mooversion+' from Google';
    // show the msg in two different ways (just because)
    document.write(msg);
    alert(msg);
  </script>
</body>
```

How it works...

There are several competing factors that go into the decision to use a direct load or dynamic load via `google.load()`:

- ▶ Are we loading more than one library?
- ▶ Are our visitors using other sites that include this dynamic load?
- ▶ Can our page benefit from parallel loading?
- ▶ Do we need to provide a secure environment?

There's more...

If we are only loading one library, a direct load or local load will almost assuredly benchmark faster than a dynamic load. However, this can be untrue when browser accelerator techniques, most specifically *browser caching*, come into play. If our web server is sending no-cache headers, then dynamic load, or even direct load, as opposed to a local load, will allow the browser to cache the Google code and reduce our page load time. If our page is making a number of requests to our web server, it may be possible to have the browser waiting on a response from the server. In this instance, parallel loading from another website can allow those requests that the browser can handle in parallel to continue during such a delay.

We need to also take a look at how secure websites function with non-secure, external includes.

Many of us are familiar with the errors that can occur when a secure website is loaded with an external (or internal) resource that is not provided via **http**. The browser can pop up an alert message that can be very concerning and lose the confidence of our visitors. Also, it is common to have some sort of negative indicator in the address bar or in the status bar that alerts visitors that not all resources on the page are secure.

 Avoid mixing **http** and **https** resources; if using a secure site, opt for a local load of MooTools or use Google Library over HTTPS.

Injecting Hello World into an HTML DIV

Let us add an element to the HTML Document Object Model (DOM).

Getting ready

There is no oldie that is more goodie than greeting the world around us. There is an elemental power to our first Hello World, a power that proclaims, "We have the power to code syntactically correct. We have the power to change things on the screen. We have the power to accomplish business goals using this language. And, we are friendly and outgoing; 'Hello'."

How to do it...

Here is an example that demonstrates MooTools' syntax and power:

```
<script type="text/javascript" src="mootools-1.3.0.js"></script>
</head>
<body>
  <div id="mycanvas">
    Knock Knock, Who's there?
    Hello, who?
  </div>
  <script type="text/javascript">
  var whocanitbenow = 'Hello World!';
  var readymsg = 'Okay to make the magic happen?';
  if (confirm(readymsg,true,false)) {

    // sexy part:
    $('mycanvas').set('html',whocanitbenow);

  } else {
    // well, since they're being silly...
    setTimeout(fallback_plan, 1000);
  }
function fallback_plan() {
  $('mycanvas').set( 'html', 'orange you glad there is a
    backup message?');
}
  </script>
```

How it works...

So, as usual in our favorite MooTools cookbook, the alluring part is set with spacing above and below. Here is the 1, 2, 3 of what is happening in that nugget of goodness:

- We use the MooTools dollar, **$**, to select our DIV
- We use the MooTools method `set()`
- We send two arguments to `set()`

MooTools **$** has a counterpart, the double dollar sign: **$$**, which is used for sending CSS selectors and returns a multiple element **collection**.

The single **$**, originally reserved for grabbing *DOM unique*, id attributed elements takes no punctuation not already inherent in the name of the id attribute.

Using MooTools dollar not only empowers us with cross-browser compatible code to humbly abstract and replace the infamous, JavaScript built-in, `getElementById()` method to get the element, but it also **enhances** the returned object with Moo-methods like `get()` and `set()`.

Using Multiple Frameworks

It is imperative to use `document.id(<id>)` instead of its alias, `$(<id>)`, when working with multiple frameworks. Reviewing the Moo-source shows that `document.id` is used exclusively. When another framework is using the dollar syntax, MooTools attempts to sense that and not extend the object.

There's more...

The `get()` method *returns* the attribute or property value requested while the `set()` method *takes* the attribute/property argument and a value to which the property should change. In this example we could use `$('mycanvas').set('text',whocanitbenow);`. That would do the same thing as our example, since we have only altered text, but would prevent us from injecting HTML and would strip all existing HTML from our text.

We now see that our goal with this recipe is to try it out; be sure to change the *whocanitbenow* variable to something with HTML in it like this:

```
<script type="text/javascript">
  var whocanitbenow = '<strong>Hello <em>World</em></strong>!';
  var readymsg = 'Okay to make the magic happen?';
  if (confirm(readymsg,true,false)) {

  // "alluring" part:
  $('mycanvas').set('html',whocanitbenow);

  } else {
    // well, since they're being silly...
    setTimeout(fallback_plan, 1000);
  }
  function fallback_plan() {
    $('mycanvas').set( 'html', 'orange you glad there is a
      backup message?');
  }
</script>
```

See also

For more information on CSS selectors see
http://www.w3.org/TR/CSS2/selector.html.

Storing a list of names in an array of values

In this recipe we will learn how to use a standard data structure called an Array to store a list of names or values.

Getting ready

To create an array, a storage element that holds a list of values, elements, or objects, we use the raw JavaScript Array object to define a literal array `var myarray = [1, 2, 'my 3rd value'];`. In our example, we first declare our array; it is in an empty state, then we call upon either raw JavaScript's `push()` array object method or MooTools' extension of the array native `include()`, based on the ternary output, to add our string value to the array.

How to do it...

Add items to an array. Allow or disallow the addition of duplicate items with a switch in the form.

```
<script type="text/javascript" src="mootools-1.3.0.js"></script>
</head>
<body>
  <form action="" method="get">
    <input type="text" id="myitem"/>
      Ignore if already in the array?
    <input type="checkbox" id="unique"/>
    <input type="button" id="mybutton"
      value="Add  This"
      onclick="store_item_in_array();"/>
  </form>

  <script type="text/javascript">

    // declare the array
    var myarray = [];

    // an array-dedicated utility function to add elements
    function store_item_in_array() {
      // use the $ object to get element with id "myitem"
      var myitem = $('myitem').value;
      // ternary operators can save a lot of space
      var ischecked = $('unique').get('checked');
      var unique = (ischecked)  ?  1  :  0;
      if (!unique) {
        // (A) add an item to an array with raw JavaScript
        myarray.push(myitem);
      } else {
        // (B) add an item to an array, but make it moonique
        myarray.include(myitem);
      }
      alert('Length  of  Array:  '+myarray.length);
    }
  </script>
```

How it works...

Much like **$**, arrays are infused with methods that extend their capability. This snippet calls the JavaScript inherent `push()`, which post-pends the single argument to the array, like this: `var myarray.push('myvalue');`.

> **NOTE:** The JavaScript array object will hold much more than string values: it can hold integers, objects, even other array objects to create multi-dimensional arrays!

MooTools has further extended the array prototype by adding new, useful methods. The method used here is called `include()`, which works identically both in syntax and in function to `push()`; however, it adds a duplicate value check to the incoming argument. If one or more values present are matched, the function does not add a value to the array.

There's more

We should open up the uncompressed version of our MooTools and search for the phrase "include". We can quickly see how `include()` is an abstraction that enhances `push()`.

Looping over an array of names and saying "Hello" to all of them

In this recipe we will be looping over an array of names and saying "Hello" to each of them.

Getting ready

To initialize our list of names, we look to the United States' President, Barack Obama, who did an interview in 2008 with *Rolling Stone* magazine and mentioned the oldies musicians found on his iPod. Let's loop over that list and say, 'Hello' to each of them.

How to do it...

Use literal JavaScript array definition to put the array values in an object array, `var obamas_ oldies = ['Stevie Wonder', 'a lot of Bob Dylan', 'a lot of Rolling Stones', 'a lot of Miles Davis', 'John Coltrane'];`. *Using either of the other types of array object instantiation syntax would not affect this example.*

```
<script type="text/javascript" src="mootools-1.3.0.js"></script>
</head>
<body>

    Hello  Bulletin  Board:<br/>
```

```
<div id="hello_board"></div>

<script type="text/javascript">
  var oldies = ['Stevie Wonder', 'a lot of Bob Dylan',
    'a lot of Rolling Stones', 'a lot of Miles Davis',
    'John Coltrane'];
  var hb = $('hello_board');

  // iterating an array using a bound function
  obamas_oldies.each(
    function(oldie,  index){
      hb.set('html',hb.get('html')+'<br/>Hello '+oldie+',
        you are number '+index+' on the Obama playlist!');
    }
  );

</script>
```

How it works...

Once we have an array of values, it is inevitable that we will need to loop over them. Iterating through array values is made *mooch* more simple by our JavaScript abstraction layer's iteration methods, each() and forEach(), which extend when a browser does not have, built-in, a forEach() iterator. The two methods are identical.

In the example, for effect, a line break is separating the each() opening and the beginning of the mandatory first argument, the callback function. There does not need to be a space here; usually, programmers write the **first line** (including the optional secondary argument) as such:

```
obamas_oldies.each(function(oldie, index){
```

On the final line, the closing curly brace of the function and the closing parenthesis of the argument are nearly always sandwiched together:

```
});
```

The get() and set() method of the **$**-defined DOM object allow us to inject the HTML message(s).

See also

When we return to the MooTools online documentation to learn more about the get() and set() methods, we really prepare ourselves to become MooTool aficionados, ready at a moment's notice to help a friend or coworker with their Moo-predicaments.

Doing more with a list of names by creating an object

Objects, like arrays, are used to store information; however, they can be used to also store functionality. When a value is stored in an object, it is referred to as a property. When functionality is embedded in an object, it is called a method. This recipe shows how to use properties and methods of objects in MooTools.

Getting ready

An **object** is a reusable, client-side, storage syntax. In other words, it's like a function because we can call it from anywhere, but it is also like a miniature, temporary database, too!

 We can make a parallelism between instances of an object and rows of a database. That imagery can be furthered by likening columns, fields of the row, to **properties** of the object.

In raw JavaScript, one way to add a property to an object is with the dot operator like this: `my_object.name = 'Jay LG Johnston';`. Unfortunately, that does not allow us to reuse the object. In other words, if our code was used in another place, we would have to copy and paste the entire block.

Defining built-in functions, called **methods** on this kind of *singleton class* is possible, but our storage mechanism will only ever hold *one row*, at any given time. Our code in the singleton could not be used without copying and pasting it to other singleton objects. More explanation follows.

How to do it...

Instead of creating our object as a single instance, we create a **template object** using the MooTools **Class** object. This abstraction allows us to use a more familiar syntax for creating our objects.

```
<script type="text/javascript" src="mootools-1.3.0.js"></script>
</head>
<body>

    Hello Bulletin Board:<br/>
    <div id="hello_board"></div>

    <script type="text/javascript">
```

```
var hb = $('hello_board');
var my_object = new Class({

  // object constructor
  initialize:  function(oldies_array){
    this.oldies  =  oldies_array;
  },

  //  object  method
  say_hello:  function()  {
    this.oldies.each(
      function(oldie,  index){
        hb.set('html',hb.get('html')+'<br/>Hello '+oldie+',
        you are number '+index+' on the playlist!');
      }
    );
    hb.set('html',hb.get('html')+'<br/>');
  }

});

var oldies = ['Stevie Wonder', 'a lot of Bob Dylan',
  'a lot of Rolling Stones', 'a lot of Miles Davis',
  'John Coltrane'];
var obama = new my_object(oldies);
obama.say_hello();

var oldies = ['George Thorogood', 'Dennis DeYoung',
  'The  Cyrkle'];
var other = new my_object(oldies);
other.say_hello();

</script>
```

How it works...

When we have a tiny storage mechanism to store our values with simple syntax, we can call internal methods on each instance of a templated object. Through code reuse like this, we can really bring value to our employers.

There's more...

This sort of code reuse is a feature of **Object Oriented Programming** (**OOP**). Let us now update our resumes for we know the basics of code reuse and must proclaim our ability to add value in the workplace.

The search engines have links to Wikipedia articles describing different design patterns in the OOP world. Knowing more about those patterns not only makes our code better but prepares us for those pesky interview questions.

Creating a pop-up alert upon clicking a DIV

Here we will learn how to use an event listener to pop up an alert box.

Getting ready

We are familiar with how to place an HTML attribute like `onmouseover` that will execute upon a user's mouse entering the space of the HTML element. This is a frequent method of creating roll-over actions for buttons on website navigation. When editing a website that has these code-heavy roll overs, it can be confusing how to alter the roll overs. They create quite a bit of code.

How to do it...

Now MooTools makes our lives easy; we see that MooTools itself is becoming an oldie-*and*-goodie. It is exciting to learn that using listeners, heretofore a jUnGlE of confusing syntax, is now as simple as calling the `addEvent()` method with which MooTools has extended our elements.

```
<script type="text/javascript" src="mootools-1.3.0.js"></script>
</head>
<body>

  <div id="my_trigger" style="width:100px; height:100px;
    border:1px solid  #BEBEBE; line-height:50px;
    text-align:center;">Click  Me</div>

  <script type="text/javascript">

  var count = 0;
  $('my_trigger').addEvent('click',function()  {
    $('my_trigger').set('html','Click  Me<br/>'+(++count));
```

```
        alert('Hello, please be aware that my_trigger has
           been clicked!');

    });

    </script>
```

How it works...

The addEvent() method takes two arguments (1) the event name and (2) the callback handler or function definition. Event names include all the common events defined by HTML; however, they each drop the "on"; for instance, instead of passing "onSubmit" as the event name, pass "submit": $('my_form').addEvent('submit',function() { return false; });.

The World Wide Web Consortium, W3C, publishes a plethora of information on events in HTML. While we might not have time to read all of it, being familiar with where it is allows us to seek out the answers to really advanced questions that will come up along the path of our development careers.

There's more...

In our example, we add an event function to my_form. Within that function we then make calls to the same element my_form. This can be reduced further by using a keyword that describes the element that is the owner of the executing function, **this**:

```
$('my_trigger').addEvent('click',function()   {
    this.set('html','Click   Me<br/>'+(++count));
. . .
```

Adding multiple event listeners to an HTML element

Listeners make an HTML element stand at the ready, waiting to do what it has been tasked with.

Getting ready

Once familiar with the built-in JavaScript and additional MooTool events that we can bind actions to, we note the addEvent() syntax from the previous recipe and move on to the more agile addEvents() syntax.

How to do it...

The syntax for adding multiple events is similar enough to adding a single event that one could nearly guess it. Look at this example to see how intuitive it is:

```
<script type="text/javascript" src="mootools-1.3.0.js"></script>
</head>
<body>
  <div id="my_trigger" style="width:100px;  height:100px;
    border:1px  solid  #BEBEBE;  line-height:100px;
    text-align:center;"></div>

  <script type="text/javascript">

    $('my_trigger').addEvents({
      'mouseover':  function()  {
        this.set('html','MouseOver!');
      },
      'mouseout':  function()  {
        this.set('html','MouseOut!');
      },
      'click':  function()  {
        var width = (this.getStyle('border-width').
          toInt()==1) ? '5px'  : '1px';
        this.setStyle('border-width',width);
      }
    });
  </script>
```

How it works...

The syntax for adding multiple events is very similar to that of adding a single event. Remembering that addEvent() takes the event name and the function to execute, we can easily see that addEvents() takes the same two arguments, only in hashed form so that multiple event names can have individual functions applied to them.

There's more...

In our example, we have defined three events to listen for: onmouseover, onmouseout, and onclick. Remove the "on" prefix for events when using these functions.

MooTools adds two important events that help to solve the event bubbling dilemma where each parent and children both report events causing them to fire more times than one would expect: `mouseenter` and `mouseleave`. These events were originally proprietary to Internet Explorer.

New to what we have seen so far in the book is `Element.setStyle()`. This method, along with its sibling, `Element.getStyle()`, do just as they suggest. They help us to get and set style properties. The syntax parallels that of `addEvent()` and `addEvents()`.

Our goal for this chapter is to sit down and remove a lot of cut-and-paste code from one of our projects and replace with a very slick, object oriented roll over based on this recipe. Let's go!

Dragging an HTML element

HTML can be moved around on a page with a click-and-hold while moving the mouse.

Getting ready

MooTools has two libraries: Core and More. The Core contains code that is always used for every MooTools application and is found at `http://mootools.net/core`. There are many goodies that are oldie or otherwise in the MooTools More library: `http://mootools.net/more`.

In a previous recipe we profiled the sizes of different MooTools versions. There are different versions of MooTools More; nevertheless, we will be profiling only different _selections for download_ of the 1.3.0 MooTools More library:

mootools_core-more-1.3.0.js	328K
mootools_core-more-1.3.0c.js	224K
mootools_core-more-nolocale-1.3.0.js	217K
mootools_core-more-nolocale-1.3.0c.js	137K

In the actual oldies, when 14.4K dial-up connections rocked our Mozilla Netscape worlds, 137K was enough of a boat anchor to cause a visitor to leave and never return. Fortunately, in this day of 500K _skip-this-preview_ splash pages, if we are truly providing a fresh user interface, we may be forgiven for an extra 137K of library. Still, it is to everyone's benefit to selectively choose, from the MooTools More download page, _only **the More classes needed once a site goes into production**_.

In development, though, our scope may change rapidly, so let us get the whole shebang. One consideration we might make for development, to reduce our own code-refresh loop time, is to not include the **Locale** functions. Shown earlier are the compressed ("c.js") and non-compressed versions of the full More and the More minus the **Locale** functions.

How to do it...

```html
<!-- we have to have the core, always -->
  <script type="text/javascript" src="mootools-1.3.0.js"></script>

  <!-- we need the more, with the core! -->
  <script type="text/javascript" src="mootools-more-nolocale-
    1.3.0.js"></script>

</head>
<body>

    <div id="my_trigger" style="width:100px; height:100px;
      border:1px solid #BEBEBE; line-height:50px;
      text-align:center;">Drag Me</div>

    <script type="text/javascript">

    // show how easy it is to make a dragging object
    var movin_object = new Drag.Move('my_trigger');

    </script>
```

How it works...

Defining a `Drag` object is as simple as passing an element ID to the method `Drag.move()`. That method also takes a second argument, which is an object that itself can have properties and *anonymous functions*, which become the definitions of methods that enhance the individual dragging object.

There's more...

Events available to dragging objects include:

- onSnap
- onComplete
- onDrop
- onEnter
- onLeave

See also

The MooTools site has several nice demonstrations of the `Drag` class. We are really familiar with those so that we have the best footing for expanding our own ideas on how to use them, *not* so that we can capitalize upon them in an as-is state. The link to the website is `http://mootools.net/demos/`.

Understanding MooTools ubiquitous anonymous functions

Functions have names, but anonymous functions do not; MooTools uses them everywhere.

 Anonymous functions are one-time use like disposable lighters. In MooTools, we use them to one-time define a method; reusable disposable functions!

Getting ready

To define and call an anonymous function raw JavaScript wraps a function in parentheses:

```
(function(){document.title=location.href;alert('done');})();
```

Nothing is returned, and the function is not assigned to a function identifier; when the **()** function syntax is appended, the function self-executes.

How to do it...

MooTools' use differs slightly in that we will pass this anonymous function as an argument to a MooTool object and bind it to an identifier; the anonymous syntax does not change.

```
<script type="text/javascript" src="mootools-1.3.0.js"></script>
</head>
<body>

    <div  id="my_trigger"  style="width:100px;  height:100px;
      border:1px  solid  #BEBEBE;  line-height:50px;
      text-align:center;">Click  Me</div>

    <script type="text/javascript">
// (A) would change title, alerts done in true lisp style
//(function(){document.title=location.href;alert('done');})();
```

```
// (B) saves the anonymous function in a variable
   var af = (function(){
   document.title=location.href;
   alert('done');
   });

// (C) "calls" the anonymous function (commented out)
//af();

// (D) returns the function (and alerts its text)
//alert($lambda(af));   // note, lambda is deprecated

// (E) binds function to the click event on my_trigger

   $('my_trigger').addEvent('click',
       af
   );

   </script>
```

How it works...

- ▶ **A** indicates a classical JavaScript style, anonymous, self-executing function.
- ▶ **B** (used in our recipe) assigns a self-executing function to an identifier.
- ▶ **C** in raw JavaScript would *call* the self-executing function.
- ▶ **D** demonstrates deprecated usage of MooTools' **$lambda** object.
- ▶ **E** (used in our recipe) passes the function to be bound to click events.

There's more...

Speaking in a strictly semantic world where anonymity is not compromised by that golden oldie *1984* and Orson Wells' cameras and dictatorial fiction, an anonymous function cannot be called more than once; it is defined, executed, and lost. Assigning it to an identifier would, in a pure discourse, render it no longer anonymous. Verily, the point of a recipe on anonymous functions is but to aid us in our understanding behind the science on how functions are passed to objects and then later executed as methods. Read up on more about what anonymous functions are on your favorite wiki site and send the author assertively argumentative proof as to the gamut of viewpoints regarding this subject.

Making an Ajax call

Getting ready

Asynchronous JavaScript and XML (Ajax) saves time by updating a page without refreshing it completely. Ajax has been around for a long time, with varied limits of browser support. It is safe to say that Google is most guilty of showing the world how easy it is to use.

How to do it...

Now with the MooTools abstraction layer's **Request** object, Ajax is child's play.

```
    <script type="text/javascript" src="mootools-1.3.0.js"></script>
</head>
<body>
    <form action="" method="get">
      <input type="button" id="mybutton" value="Ajax!"

          onclick="ajax_it();"/>

    </form>
    <script type="text/javascript">
var myJax  =  new  Request({
      url:  '?',
      onSuccess:  function(response)  {

   alert('Success! Here is the response: ' +response);

      }
});
function ajax_it()  {

      myJax.send();

}
    </script>
```

How it works...

Switch the `url` property to that of the script that will process the Ajax request. Like any good recipe, it is important to switch out ingredients as the chef's needs arise, for instance, artificial sweeteners for sugar. In this snippet, the `url` variable, or to be more semantically correct, `property` of the `myJax` object is currently set to `?`. This probably only has purpose in this academic setting. The usage in this case causes this page to request itself, and the result is that the page calls its own URL and displays the resulting source code.

There's more...

One great example of how to use Ajax to make our web pages more friendly is in conjunction with a user sign-up form. It can be frustrating for users to submit their form only to find out their desired username is in use.

Program the sign-up form's input field to make an Ajax call `onkeyup`. The returning value would be a Boolean that could be used to notify the user whether their choice was available or in use.

See also

Chapter 5, Mr. Clean Uses Ajax: Remote Asynchronous Calls is complete with `Request()`, `Request.HTML`, and `Request.JSON` examples.

2
Switching Paddles Midstream: Changing HTML After Page Load

The *Web 2.0* movement got into full swing as developers everywhere learned that users were human and desired ergonomic, friendly interfaces. You will find in this chapter ideas on:

- ▸ Finding and collecting elements in the DOM
- ▸ Adding and removing elements in the DOM
- ▸ Introducing new and styling existing elements in the DOM

The HTML DOM is a tree of tags. The root of the tree is the `<html></html>` tag itself. All tags within this tree belong to it; furthermore, tags within those tags belong to those tags.

 We are all comfortable with viewing the source of an HTML document. Please note that any changes to the HTML after a page loads will not be apparent when viewing the source.

Finding an element by its ID attribute

This cross-browser method allows us to quickly get a "handle" on our HTML element.

How to do it...

If we imagined a world where we could grab an element with a simple and easy-to-remember syntax **just by sending the element's ID attribute**, we would be dreaming of MooTools.

```
<script type="text/javascript"
    src="mootools-1.3.0.js"></script>
</head>
<body>
  <div id="my_trigger"
    style="width:100px; height:100px;
    border:1px solid #BEBEBE;
    line-height:50px; text-align:center;">You Found Me!</div>
  <noscript>JavaScript is disabled.</noscript>
```

 Always include the NOSCRIPT tag, which is omitted going forward only to save space.

```
<script  type="text/javascript">
// raw javascript's familiar method, not cross-browser use
// var my_element = document.getElementByID('my_target');
//  MooTools uses the $ object to grab elements by ID
var my_element = $('my_trigger');
var my_element_text = my_element.get('text');
alert(my_element_text);
</script>
```

 Always include the closing BODY and HTML tags. Also omitted going forward.

```
</body>
</html>
```

How it works...

When we use raw JavaScript to get a handle on an element, we either depend on the browser to match our code, or we have to write a mess of browser compatibility to be sure that our user has a browser that supports the JavaScript implementation that we are writing for. MooTools abstracts that cross-browser nightmare and gives us the dollar object $(), an alias for document.id().

Starting with version 1.2, MooTools began to use `document.id()` to grab elements by ID. This allows MooTools to play nice with other frameworks that extend using the dollar syntax. When using multiple frameworks, do not use the `$()` alias for `document.id()`.

Pass the dollar or `document.id()` object the ID for the element to grab, and the object returned is a MooTools-extended object ready to do our bidding through **Element** methods.

In this example, we use the method `get()`, which takes a single argument, the property of the object to return. We then alert the var `my_element_text` to the screen using the raw JavaScript `alert()` function.

There's more...

This recipe can be easily recreated with a single, easy-to-understand one-liner:

```
alert($('my_trigger').get('text'));
```

Finding a group of elements by their class attribute

Collections of HTML elements may be handled as a group.

Getting ready

A favorite trick is to turn the **option** elements of a **select** on and off. Using various collections of elements, this is a snap in MooTools.

How to do it...

Use ID attributes to affect unique elements: `$('my_single_target')`, and use class attributes to affect groups of elements: `$$('.my_target_class')`.

```
      <script type="text/javascript" src="mootools-1.3.0.js"></script>
   </head>
   <body>
      <form action="javascript:" method="get">
         Choose an Animal:<br/>
         <select id="animal">
            <option value="">Select Animal</option>
            <option value="cat">Cat</option>
            <option value="dog">Dog</option>
            <option value="pig">Pig</option>
         </select>
```

```
    // some browsers do not fire select onchange
    // until focus changes
    <input type="button" value="Select Animal"/>
    <br/><br/>
    <select id="animal_items">
      <!-- cat options -->
      <option class="nopeek cat" value="1">Ball of String</option>
      <option class="nopeek cat" value="2">Fake Mouse</option>
      <option class="nopeek cat" value="3">Catnip (mmm)</option>
      <!-- dog options -->
      <option class="nopeek dog" value="4">Juicy Bone</option>
      <option class="nopeek dog" value="5">Bouncy Ball</option>
      <option class="nopeek dog" value="6">Rope w/ Handle</option>
      <!-- pig options -->
      <option class="nopeek pig" value="7">Mud</option>
      <option class="nopeek pig" value="8">Slop</option>
      <option class="nopeek pig" value="9">Water Hose</option>
    </select>
  </form>
  <noscript>JavaScript is disabled.</noscript>
  <script type="text/javascript">

  // get a collection of elements so we can hide them onchange
  var all = $$('.nopeek');

  all.setStyle('display','none');

  $('animal').addEvent('change',function pare_options() {
    all.setStyle('display','none');
    var animal_chosen = $('animal').get('value');
    $$('.'+animal_chosen).setStyle('display','block');
  });
  </script>
```

How it works...

Our first **select** has a group of choices where each value represents a class that is given to groups of **option** elements in the second drop-down menu. When the first widget is changed, the **onChange** event calls the bound anonymous function and uses the class `all` to turn off the visibility of all option elements then uses the class value chosen to pare down the selection options.

There's more...

When dealing with **select** elements, be prepared for browser quirks especially the actual timing of the **onChange** event. Here we have a fake button used solely to cause our user to change the focus off the element so that we are certain the event fires.

Moving an element with a particular ID

Once an element is under our beck and call, we can send it somewhere else on the page.

How to do it...

In our HTML sketch, we are pretending to vote for the greater of two, very influential people. Each influence is represented by an element on the page with a unique ID attribute. Moving elements around when we know their unique ID attribute value is simple with the MooTool infused `Element::inject()` method.

```
<script type="text/javascript" src="mootools-1.3.0.js"></script>
</head>
<body>
  <form action="javascript:" method="get">
    Choose the greatest influence of the Internet:<br/>
    <select id="influence">
      <option value="">Vote Now:</option>
      <option value="bill">Bill</option>
      <option value="linus">Linus</option>
    </select>
    <input type="button" value="..."/>
  </form>
  <img id="bill" src="bill_gates.bmp" alt="Bill"/>
  <img id="linus" src="linus_torvalds.bmp" alt="Linus"/>
  <div>
    <h1>Voted Greatest Influencer of the Internet: </h1>
  </div>
  <div id="my_target" style="width:150px; height:150px;
    border:1px solid #BEBEBE; line-height:50px;
    text-align:center;"></div>

  <noscript>JavaScript is disabled.</noscript>
  <script type="text/javascript">
  $('influence').addEvent('change',function() {
    var id_to_move = $('influence').value;
```

```
        // use MooTools Element::inject() to move an item
        $(id_to_move).inject('my_target');

        // we can't have people voting twice
        $('influence').removeEvents();
    });
    </script>
</body>
</html>
```

How it works...

The `inject()` method takes two parameters, though only one is mandatory. The requisite, first argument is the HTML element ID of the target canvas in which we wish to inject our element. The second argument that we may send is the keyword location of where we wish to inject the element relative to any existing content in the target element.

Appropriate values for the second argument of `inject()` include:

- `after`
- `before`
- `top`
- `bottom` (default value)

Two of the numerous methods that are similar to this are `replace()` and `grab()`. To remove all existing content, use the former. To reverse the inclusion syntax, use `grab()` thusly:

`$('my_target').grab('bill').`

There's more...

Moving elements on a page is the cornerstone to providing a user-friendly environment. However, it is very important that we always do this with caution. Moving an element when the user is not expecting it can disorient them or even make them think the page is malfunctioning. Also, be sure to take those with sight disabilities into consideration. Not all screen-reading software will properly notify a non-sighted visitor that page elements have changed!

The industry *best practice* for non-sighted visitors and page modifications on the fly: if the modification happens further down the page from the triggering element, screen reading software will not have read to the point of modification. It is okay to modify in this way.

Modifying the page above or prior to the triggering element is not okay without sending some sort of tactile feedback to the user that the page should be refreshed.

Moving a group of elements using their HTML tag

Feel the managerial power as we move a little army of elements to their new position in our HTML.

Getting ready

When working with a complex form, all methods of grabbing elements are useful. We may wish to loop over all select values or option elements. There could be business requirements for the form to validate each type of element a certain way.

How to do it...

Often the gaming industry propels code development more than the business community. Games require flexible code that can be written with a minimum of syntax. Here is a recipe that might give us some ideas on how a word game could be created.

```html
    <script type="text/javascript" src="mootools-1.3.0.js"></script>
</head>
<body>
  <p><span>The </span> Fox jumped over the lazy dog.</p>
  <p>Jack and Jill went up one
    <span>hill </span> and down another.</p>
  <p>By any other name, this
    <span>rose </span> is still a rose.</p>
  <p>The superhero towered
    <span>high </span> above all others.</p>
  <p>You will find the culprit
    <span>over </span> there.</p>
  <p>We all know
    <span>the </span> ways to write good code.</p>
  <p>The rain fell mainly upon the green
    <span>trees</span> of Spain.</p>
  <p>Sentences should end with a period,
    <span>. </span> right?</p>

  <form action="" method="get">
    <input id="my_trigger" type="button" value="Go!"/>
```

```
</form>
<hr/>
<h1 id="my_new_sentence"></h1>

<script type="text/javascript">

// for effect, grab the elements before moving them
var my_elements_to_move = $$('span');

$('my_trigger').addEvent('click',function() {
  // move the element group by tag
  my_elements_to_move.inject('my_new_sentence');
});
</script>
```

How it works...

The *double dollar* object, $$ () takes a Cascading Style Sheet (CSS) selector, which can be a tag, class, descendant operator, or anything the CSS specification allows.

With this type of simple markup where we do not even need classes or ID attributes, the code and resulting canvas text are easy to read and work with.

See also

Being sure we know where to find information on the actual CSS specifications is important, let us take a brief look at the World Wide Web Consortium, W3C's website: http://www.w3.org/Style/CSS/ or http://www.w3.org/TR/css3-selectors/#selectors.

Removing an element by ID

Ready to give an element the axe? Send it to "File 13" by removing it from the page.

Getting ready

There are only four things that can be done with data. It can be Created, Read, Updated, and Deleted: *CRUD*. It was once thought that the alternative to this was to *Create, Read, Alter, and Purge* data, but we then realized that this alternative idea was *CRAP*.

Be prepared for two examples in one. The first shows a novice approach to handling actions in JavaScript. Then the second shows an industry best-practice approach, one that is less intrusive into the DOM.

How to do it...

In this exercise, we delete, or *purge* an element from the HTML DOM by use of the
`destroy()` method.

```
    <script type="text/javascript" src="mootools-1.3.0.js"></script>
</head>
<body>

    <p id="s1">The Fox jumped over the lazy dog.
      <a href="#"
        onclick="javascript:delete_by_id('s1');">
        <small>DELETE THIS CRUD</small></a>
    </p>
    <p id="s2">Jack and Jill went up one hill and down another.
      <a href="#"
        onclick="javascript:delete_by_id('s2');">
        <small>DELETE THIS CRUD</small></a>
    </p>
    <p id="s3">By any other name, this rose is still a rose.
      <a href="#"
        onclick="javascript:delete_by_id('s3');">
        <small>DELETE THIS CRUD</small></a>
    </p>
    <p id="s4">The superhero towered high above all others.
      <a href="#"
        onclick="javascript:delete_by_id('s4');">
        <small>DELETE THIS CRUD</small></a>
    </p>

    <noscript>JavaScript is disabled.</noscript>
    <script type="text/javascript">
    function delete_by_id(id) {

      // when we know the id, it's very easy to get rid of it
      $(id).destroy();

      if ($$('p').length===0) {
        alert('Eegads!  We've deleted the entire universe!  Undo!');
        location.href="?undo";
      }
    }
    </script>
```

How it works...

Removing an object by ID is pretty simple; we just use the syntax $(my_element).
destroy(). If we wish to only remove the *contents* of an object we use $(my_element).
empty(). We may also use dispose() which will *return the element* for client-side storage.
That way *it can be injected back into the DOM* later if the need arises.

There's more...

> *Unobtrusive JavaScript* is a best industry practice. We always notify our
> users that they may have JavaScript disabled as one small step in writing
> unobtrusive JavaScript. The javascript: keyword included inside an
> href attribute may be commonplace; but instead, let us help our users,
> by attaching a *listener* to fire the appropriate function and keep our
> JavaScript unobtrusive.

One solution for attaching a listener in this recipe is completely removing the A tags and
adding ID attributes to the SMALL tags to create a listener on the element that will respond,
unobtrusively to the click event.

```
<script type="text/javascript" src="mootools-1.3.0.js"></script>
</head>
<body>
  <p id="s1">The Fox jumped over the lazy dog.
    <small id="d1">DELETE THIS CRUD</small>
  </p>
  <p id="s2">Jack and Jill went up one hill and down another.
    <small id="d2">DELETE THIS CRUD</small>
  </p>
  <p id="s3">By any other name, this rose is still a rose.
    <small id="d3">DELETE THIS CRUD</small>
  </p>
  <p id="s4">The superhero towered high above all others.
    <small id="d4">DELETE THIS CRUD</small>
  </p>

  <script type="text/javascript">
  // remember that double dollar takes a css selector
  $$('small').addEvent('click',function() {
    // the IDs are conveniently congruent
    var my_id_2_delete = this.id.replace('d','s');
    delete_by_id(my_id_2_delete);
  });
```

```
function delete_by_id(id) {
  // when we know the id, it's very easy to get rid of it
  $(id).destroy();

}
</script>

<!-- our delete links should look like links, yay! -->
<style type="text/css">
  small { cursor: pointer; color: #00F; }
</style>
```

When using unobtrusive JavaScript, it will often be left to us to properly style elements. In this unobtrusive example, the SMALL elements are styled to appear as links.

See also

There are a lot of great articles on unobtrusive JavaScript that can be dug up using any good search engine. When we are familiar with those, we are not only going to write code that works better, but also write code that is easier to maintain!

Removing a group of elements using CSS selectors

Have an offending group of HTML elements? This task will obliterate them in one fell swoop.

Getting ready

CSS Selectors are used in styling to grab specific elements. This makes them a great way to also identify and group elements of our HTML DOM. Remember, grab single elements by their ID attributes; those are always unique on a page.

How to do it...

Grab *groups* of elements by CSS selector, most frequently by class. In our example, we use both class and tag CSS syntax to group together elements that we will remove.

```
<script type="text/javascript" src="mootools-1.3.0.js"></script>
</head>
<body>

  <p class="remove"><span>The </span>
    Fox jumped over the lazy dog.</p>
```

```
<p class="remove">Jack and Jill went up one <span>hill </span>
   and down another.</p>
<p>By any other name, this <span>rose </span>
   is still a rose.</p>
<p>The superhero towered <span>high </span>
   above all others.</p>
<p class="nomove">You will find the culprit <span>over </span>
   there.</p>
<p class="nomove">We all know <span>the </span>
   ways to write good code.</p>
<div>The rain fell mainly upon the green <span>trees</span>
   of Spain.</div>
<br/>
<div>Sentences should end
   <span>with a period, right?</span></div>
<br/>
<form action="javascript:" method="get">
   <input id="my_trigger" type="button" value="Go!"/>
</form>

<style type="text/css">
   p span, div span { color:#F00; }
   p.remove { font-weight:bold; }
</style>

<script type="text/javascript">
// for effect, grab the elements before moving them
var my_elements_to_REmove = $$('p.remove span');

$('my_trigger').addEvent('click',function() {

   // move the element group by tag
   my_elements_to_REmove.destroy();

});
</script>
```

How it works...

The styles defined cause our paragraph elements with class remove to be bold. This
helps us see what is happening. Our CSS selector is p.remove span, so all SPAN tags
found within a paragraph tag with class remove are selected and grouped into the variable
my_elements_to_REmove. We then use a click listener on my_trigger to fire the destroy
method on this group of elements.

There's more...

Being familiar with CSS selectors is quite **crucial** in our work with MooTools. Always remember the rule-of-thumb:

- Single elements: grab using `$('my_id')`
- Multiple elements: grab using `$$('#my .css_selector')`

We can bone up on CSS selectors at W3Schools' **excellent** syntax and tutorial section `http://www.w3schools.com/css/css_syntax.asp`.

Adding an element with a unique ID

We will inject new blood into our message by adding a new HTML element to the page.

Getting ready

The `Element` class deals with methods such as `inject()` and `destroy()`. There are also classes for `String` and `Number` among others. When faced with a need to add an element with a unique ID attribute, we turn to `String.uniqueID()`. This method uses `Date.now()` to return a string that will be, invariably, unique.

How to do it...

Note that to make a copy of our existing `my_target` we use `Element.clone()`.

```
    <script type="text/javascript" src="mootools-1.3.0.js"></script>
</head>
<body>
  <form action="javascript:" method="get">
    <input type="button" value="Unique Me!"/>
  </form>

  <div id="my_target" style="width:150px; height:150px;
    border:1px solid #BEBEBE; line-height:50px;
    text-align:center; float:left;"></div>

  <noscript>JavaScript is disabled.</noscript>
  <script type="text/javascript">
    $$('input[type=button]').addEvent('click',function() {
      var element_to_copy = $('my_target');                 // A
      var my_target_id = element_to_copy.get('id');         // B
```

```
        var my_unique_id = String.uniqueID();                 // C

        var my_cloned_target = element_to_copy.clone();        // D
        my_cloned_target.set('id',my_unique_id);               // E
        my_cloned_target.set('text',my_unique_id);             // F
        my_cloned_target.inject(element_to_copy,'after');
      });
    </script>
  </body>
  </html>
```

How it works...

In line *C*, we use the `String` class to initialize a unique value in `my_unique_id`. There are many methods such as `uniqueID()` that are available to this class like `test()`, `trim()`, `capitalize()`, and `toInt()` to name a few.

There's more...

There are several shortcuts that we could take in this recipe.

  ▸ Combine A and B in our example like this:

```
my_target_id = $('my_target').get('id');
```

  ▸ If we combine A and B, update D:

```
var my_cloned_target = $('my_target').clone();
```

  ▸ The method `set()` can take an object of properties to merge E and F:

```
my_cloned_target.set({'id':my_unique_id, 'text':my_unique_id});
```

  ▸ Finally, we could chain the actions for `my_cloned_target`:

```
my_cloned_target.set({'id':my_unique_id,
    'text':my_unique_id}).inject($('my_target'),'after');
```

  ▸ In fact, the only line that cannot be collapsed is the initialization of the unique ID:

```
$$('input[type=button]').addEvent('click',function() {
  var my_unique_id = String.uniqueID();
  //C
  $('my_target').clone().set({'id':my_unique_id,
    'text':my_unique_id}).inject($('my_target'),'after');
});
```

Cloning an object does remove the ID attribute, though that does not help us if we need unique IDs for any reason. The ID attribute must always be unique in the DOM. We may note that Firefox internally tracks each ID uniquely; however, Internet Explorer and others will not be so forgiving. **Keep ID attributes unique!**

Adding a group of elements with incremented IDs

When we need a new group of elements but each must be unique on the page, this trick works well.

Getting ready

Classes define groups of elements. When making a group of radio buttons, we give them all the same NAME attribute. When making a group of elements, we give them all the same class. But what happens when we need to be able to identify members of that group individually?

How to do it...

It is necessary for each member to have its own unique ID attribute. We could generate that using `String.uniqueID()`; yet, sometimes an incrementing ID scheme can be helpful and easier to read.

```
    <script type="text/javascript" src="mootools-1.3.0.js"></script>
</head>
<body>

  <form action="" method="get">
    <input id="create" type="button"
      value="Increment Radio Buttons"/>
    <input id="extract" type="button"
      value="Get ID of Selected Radio"/>
    <br/>
    <div class="animals">
      Cat<br/>
      My Favorite <input class="rb" type="radio" name="favorite"
        value="Cat"/>
      <div class="sam-i-am"></div>
    </div>
    <div class="animals">
      Dog<br/>
      My Favorite <input class="rb" type="radio" name="favorite"
        value="Dog"/>
```

```
          <div class="sam-i-am"></div>
        </div>
        <div class="animals">
          Pig<br/>
          My Favorite <input class="rb" type="radio" name="favorite"
            value="Pig"/>
          <div class="sam-i-am"></div>
        </div>
      </form>

      <style type="text/css">
      .animals {
        width:150px; border:1px solid #BEBEBE; line-height:50px;
        text-align:center; float:left; margin-right:10px;
      }
      </style>

      <script type="text/javascript">
        $('extract').setStyle('visibility','hidden');
        $('create').addEvent('click', function() {
          // this is only meant to be fired once
          this.setStyle('visibility','hidden');
          $('extract').setStyle('visibility','visible');

          // A
          // create unique ids that increment
          $$('.rb').forEach(function(el,index) {
            el.set('id','favorite_'+index);
          });

        });
        $('extract').addEvent('click', function() {
          var myid = 0;
          // have sam tell who he is (if selected)
          $$('.rb').forEach(function(el) {
            if(el.get('checked')!==false) {
              // the incrementer here will help us know
              // which span to populate
              myid = el.get('id').replace('favorite_','');
            }
          });

          // B
          // take advantage of our incrementing pattern
```

```
$$('.sam-i-am').forEach(function(el,index) {
  el.set('text','');
  if (index===myid.toInt()) el.set('text',
    'My ID: favorite_'+myid);
});

});
</script>
```

How it works...

During the `forEach()` iterator, we use the `index` argument passed in by the MooTools framework to build a unique ID that is user friendly: `favorite_[index]`. That is visible in code block A. Then in code block B, we take advantage of that simplicity of naming by using a secondary, parallel incrementing sibling, the `sam-i-am` class DIV group.

Though this recipe took a lot of leg work to set up, the idea is clear. Incrementing ID values can allow us to more easily get control over our DOM and find the elements that we need quickly and with less coding.

There's more...

 It is often said but frequently ignored; ID attributes *MUST* be unique in the DOM!

The text injection of the `My ID: favorite_[myid]` phrase, to show the auto-increment ID selected, is necessary to display this seemingly intangible addition of the ID attributes. There is a way to see the DOM change midstream: use a live-DOM inspector to watch how our radio elements' ID attributes are added in a unique, incrementing fashion, then accessed via a patterned reconstruction via a sibling element. Many use the Firefox plugin called *Firebug* to inspect their DOM in real time.

See also

Everyone enjoys a simple explanation from an expert source; read what Mozilla says about the ID attribute's unique properties in the DOM.

```
https://developer.mozilla.org/en/DOM/element.id.
```

Styling the text within an element

We are often faced with a reason to style text on-the-fly using client-side code. MooTools makes that quite elementary with concepts found prominent in this very recipe!

Getting ready

Prepare to make the text in our SPAN stand out: by making it **bold**.

How to do it...

It is possible to set the styles of any text element quickly and easily.

```
    <script type="text/javascript" src="mootools-1.3.0.js"></script>
</head>
<body>

  <form action="" method="get">
    <input id="go_bold" type="button" value="Bold Oscar"/>
    <input id="go_div" type="button" value="Set Oscar Apart"/>
  </form>
  <br/>
  <div>Every great man nowadays has his disciples,
    and it is always Judas who writes the biography.
    <span id="quote_author">Oscar Wilde</span></div>

  <script type="text/javascript">
  $('go_bold').addEvent('click', function() {

    // set a style property of an element
    $('quote_author').setStyle('font-weight','bold');

  });
  $('go_div').addEvent('click', function() {

    // use an object to set many style properties at once
    $('quote_author').setStyles({
      'display': 'block',
      'text-decoration': 'underline',
      'font-style': 'italic',
      'font-size': '18px',
      'margin': '5px 0 0 5px'
    });

  });
  </script>
```

How it works...

The `Element.setStyle()` method takes two parameters, the style property to alter and the new value for the property. In this example, we also use `Element.setStyles()`, which will take an object that can alter many style properties in one fell swoop.

There's more...

The CSS style specification is huge; imagine the power that we have *on-the-fly* when we can change styles of any element on the page, most particularly in response to something the client user has done. Now we have interaction *and* style in doing it!

Styling the borders of a group of elements

In this recipe, we'll see how to use one style declaration phrase to alter any group of selected elements.

Getting ready

When a group of elements must have borders, we can style them all with just one call. Just as we apply styles to a single element through the `Element.setStyle()` and `Element.setStyles()` methods, our groups of elements can be styled just as easily.

How to do it...

This example demonstrates the changing of a single property with `setStyle()` as well as the changing of multiple style properties with the `setStyles()` method.

```
    <script type="text/javascript" src="mootools-1.3.0.js"></script>
</head>
<body>

  <form action="javascript:" method="get">
    <input id="go_bold" type="button"
      value="Set Borders on a Group"/>
    <input id="go_div" type="button" value="Set Authors Apart"/>
  </form>

  <br/>
  <div>Every great man nowadays has his disciples,
    and it is always Judas who writes the biography.
    <span class="quote_author">Oscar Wilde</span></div>
  <div>A hard man is good to find.
```

```
            <span class="quote_author">Mae West</span></div>
    <div>Any man who reads too much and uses his own brain
        too little falls into lazy habits of thinking.
            <span class="quote_author">Albert Einstein</span></div>
    <div>Do not be anxious about tomorrow, for tomorrow will be
        anxious for itself.
            <span class="quote_author">Jesus of Nazareth</span></div>
    <div>A successful man is one who can lay a firm foundation
        with the bricks others have thrown at him.
            <span class="quote_author">David Brinkley</span></div>

    <script type="text/javascript">
    $('go_bold').addEvent('click', function() {

        // set the borders on the div elements
        $$('div').setStyle('border','1px solid #ABABAB');

        $$('.quote_author').setStyle('font-weight','bold');
    });
    $('go_div').addEvent('click', function() {

        // use an object to set many style properties at once
        $$('.quote_author').setStyles({
            'display': 'block',
            'text-decoration': 'underline',
            'font-weight': 'bold',
            'font-style': 'italic',
            'font-size': '18px',
            'margin': '5px 0 20px 5px'
        });

    });
    </script>
```

How it works...

We use classes to grab groups of elements rather than attempting to grab each individual element by unique ID.

Creating a time clock that updates per second

We can be sure to keep our users right on time by giving them a running clock that updates every second.

Getting ready

UNIX time, measured in seconds from an arbitrary date in the 1970s, can be difficult to parse out into *human*-readable time. MooTools makes this much easier in the `MooTools MoreDate` class. There are also shortcuts for the parameter that can be passed to `Date.get()`:

 ▸ **ms/Milliseconds**
 ▸ **year/FullYear**
 ▸ **min/Minutes**
 ▸ **mo/Month**
 ▸ **sec/Seconds**
 ▸ **hr/Hours**

The seasoned coder will appreciate that all raw JavaScript date elements are available; MooTools only extends the native class.

How to do it...

Making a clock is a task that comes across our desks perennially.

```
<script type="text/javascript" src="mootools-1.3.0.js"></script>

<!-- we MUST have the MooTools more Date classes -->
<script type="text/javascript"
  src="mootools-more-1.3.0.js"></script>

</head>
<body>

  <div id="moo_clock">
    <span>0</span><span>0</span>
      <span>:</span>
    <span>0</span><span>0</span>
      <span class="blink">:</span>
    <span>0</span><span>0</span>
```

```
    </div>

    <style type="text/css">
      #moo_clock {
        position:fixed;
        border-top:3px solid #999;
        border-right:3px solid #333;
        border-bottom:3px solid #555;
        border-left:3px solid #BBB;
        background-color:#777;
        /* instead "top" and "left" */
        top:25px; left:25px;
        /* try "bottom" and "right" */
      }
      #moo_clock tr td {
          display:block;
          float:left;
          width:10px;
          text-align:center;
        border:0px;
        color:#00FF00;
      }
      #moo_clock tr td.blink {
        visibility:hidden;
      }
    </style>

    <noscript>JavaScript is disabled.</noscript>
    <script type="text/javascript">

      // create the periodic function
      function moo_time(){

        // date setup
        var js_date = new Date();
        var js_hours = js_date.get('Hours').toString().pad(2,
          '0', 'left');
        var js_minutes = js_date.get('Minutes').toString().pad(2,
          '0', 'left');
        var js_seconds = js_date.get('Seconds').toString().pad(2,
          '0', 'left');

        // switch paddles in the stream of HTML
        var tds = $$('#moo_clock span');
```

```
        // we can use a js string as an array
        var hour1 = js_hours[0];
        tds[0].set('text', hour1);

        // we can save a step in setting our time
        tds[1].set('text', js_hours[1]);
        tds[3].set('text', js_minutes[0]);
        tds[4].set('text', js_minutes[1]);
        tds[6].set('text', js_seconds[0]);
        tds[7].set('text', js_seconds[1]);

        // make the seconds' dots blink.  mmm, blink
        tds[5].toggleClass('blink');
    }

    // this is what calls the function every one second
    var moo_time_hand = moo_time.periodical(1000);

    </script>
  </body>
</html>
```

How it works...

The variable `tds` is a collection of HTML elements. The `$$` object takes a CSS selector and returns the elements. Usually, the elements are then used in a `forEach()` or `each()` iterator. We use them in this example as directly accessible elements, like those in an array. For instance, `tds[0]` represents the first SPAN element found by the CSS selector used to create `tds`. In our markup, there are eight elements in all that are selected: `tds[0]` through `tds[7]`, since this object uses a *zero-based* key structure in collecting elements. The `Element.set()` method takes two arguments, the property of the HTML element to alter and the value to which the property will be set.

There's more...

Ah, the long lost, forgotten, and hated BLINK tag. Browser implementations such as Internet Explorer dropped support for the tag somewhere along the way. It is widely accepted that misuse of the tag caused users to find it...annoying. The method `Element.toggleClass()` will add or remove a class from an element each time it is called. Our example makes use of this MooTools element method to implement a potentially viable use of blinking text.

The proverbial meat of our recipe is wrapped up quietly and discreetly in an unassuming `Function.periodical()` function that takes a minimum of one input value: the rate at which the function should periodically be called. Optionally, it can take more parameters that are then sent to the function bound by the object.

See also

 Many users suffer from conditions such as Epilepsy where **blinking text can induce seizures**. Avoid making text flicker between a frequency of 2 Hz and 55 Hz.

Check Subpart B—Technical Standards, § 1194.21 Software applications and operating systems (k) of `http://www.access-board.gov/sec508/standards.htm`.

Creating a welcome message based on a JavaScript cookie

Display an Alert "Hello, [Name]" to our visitor, with a cookie that was set some time earlier.

How to do it...

The MooTools **Cookie** class makes it surprisingly easy to create, read, access, and purge cookies. The method `Cookie.write()` takes a key, a value, and *optionally* an object of options; for instance, the option `duration` takes an integer that represents the number of days a cookie should be kept by a visitor. `Cookie.read()`, terribly simple in syntax, takes the *key* of the cookie value that we wish to read. If empty the value is, it returns false. And, of course, we could not properly purge any cookie without the handy `Cookie.dispose()` whose first parameter is identical to `read()` and second parameter will merge the passed object of options with the existing cookie object options.

```
<script type="text/javascript" src="mootools-1.3.0.js"></script>
</head>
<body>

  <form action="" method="get">
    <span id="set_cookie">
      Please enter your username:
      <input id="my_cookie_value" type="text"/>
      <input id="my_cookie_write" type="button"
        value="Write Cookie"/>
    </span>
```

```
      <input id="my_cookie_read"  type="button"
        value="Read Cookie"/>
  </form>

  <script type="text/javascript">
    // my_cookie_val will have the value of the key
    var my_cookie_val = Cookie.read('users_name');
    if (!my_cookie_val)
      $('my_cookie_read').setStyle('visibility','hidden');
    else $('my_cookie_value').set('value', my_cookie_val);
    $('my_cookie_write').addEvent('click', function() {
      // set a length of days for the cookie to be kept
      // by the user
      var days = 1;
      // get the username given by the user
      var my_cookie_val = $('my_cookie_value').get('value');

      // my_cookie_obj will have the options, key,
      // and the value in it
      var my_cookie_obj =
        Cookie.write('users_name', my_cookie_val,
          {duration: days});

      // my_cookie_read now has something to read
      $('my_cookie_read').setStyle('visibility','visible');
      $('set_cookie').setStyle('visibility','hidden');
    });
    $('my_cookie_read').addEvent('click', function() {
      var my_cookie_val = Cookie.read('users_name');
      alert('Hello '+my_cookie_val);
    });
  </script>
```

How it works...

Our final recipe in this chapter uses `Element.set()`, `Element.get()`, and
`Element.setStyle()` to read and alter properties and style properties of HTML
elements on the page, real-time. Visible, as well, are two useful examples of adding
event listeners with `Element.addEvent()`.

> Remember, you can switch paddles midstream because paddles float. Hoard
> your cookies! _Okay, just kidding,_ **share the cookies**, _we have more._

3
And on the 8th Day: Creating HTML Elements

Writing hypertext markup, HTML is like creating a house that guests will enjoy when they visit. But do guests not open and close doors? We also cook for our guests, creating items that were not previously there. In this chapter we will cook up some HTML elements in the following ways:

- Creating new elements
- Injecting new elements
- Creating new form elements

Raw JavaScript contains methods for creating and injecting HTML elements. When we use those elements, the thought may occur that the syntax for these useful methods is not quite easy to remember. The syntax for creating elements in MooTools is quite easy to follow and even easier to memorize.

Creating a DIV with a border on it

Before injecting any elements to our HTML DOM we should run HTML validation on our page. Valid HTML is crucial to having consistent, cross-browser results.

How to do it...

There is a great, artistic beauty to a syntax so simple as the constructor for the **Element** class. The first, mandatory parameter is the tag name. In this example we pass `div` in order to create a DIV tag *in memory*, not on the page...yet. The second parameter to the constructor is an object of properties to assign to the in-memory element.

```
<form action="javascript:" method="get">
  <span id="my_error"></span>
  <input id="submit" type="button" value="Submit Form"/>
</form>

<script type="text/javascript">
  $('submit').addEvent('click', function() {

    // the element constructor has a simple syntax
    my_error = new Element('div', {
      'id': 'my_error',
      'text': 'Error!',
      'style': 'border: 1px solid #F00; width:200px;'
    });

    // use element.replaces() to switch the span with a div
    my_error.replaces($('my_error'));
  // remove the error after a specified number of mseconds
  setTimeout("$('my_error').set({'text':'','style':''})",3000);
  });
</script>
```

After pressing the submit button we should see this injection for three seconds:

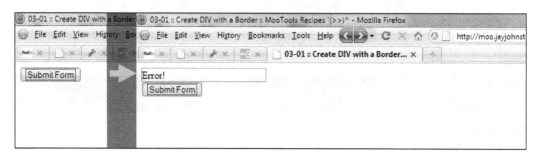

How it works...

In the second argument, where we pass an object of key/value properties to be assigned to the new element, we must pass the ID attribute or we may have trouble accessing the element later. For instance, **when we remove the error we use the ID element** along with a raw JavaScript, built-in function, `setTimeout()`.

There's more...

The **Element** method `replaces()` is used on an element, whether in-memory or on a page. Pass the element with which the replacement should happen. We can remember it this way: `my_incoming_element.replaces(my_outgoing_element)` or more concisely, `keeper.replaces(loser)`, and, yes, it is quite semantically correct! Just remember *"Keeper Fires, Loser Passes"*.

Creating an "A" tag link with linked text

During the course of user interaction, we may wish to give users an option. In the *choose-your-own-adventure* of navigating a website, choices make users feel like our interfaces are friendly. That friendliness, in turn, provides our site a stickiness that means users will tell others and come back themselves.

Getting ready

Great user interfaces are 60% planning and 40% code. We are always certain to begin with a good plan of how our users will interact. Coding too soon, before we have a good design will cause unnecessary rewrites and confusion in our code that will add to the maintenance cost of an application.

How to do it...

In this recipe, we will create a hyperlink upon user interaction to prompt secondary user interaction. *The greatest thing about programming is choosing our adventure!*

```
<div id="text" style="width:300px;font-family:fantasy">
You and the other adventurers turn the corner of the long, damp
hallway.  There is a door through which large thudding noises can be
heard and occasional light flashes can be seen around the edges of the
frame.  It smells like something is burning.</div>
<br/>
<div>
  <a href="javascript:" class="choices" id="choice_1">Open the
  Door!</a> |
```

```
        <a href="javascript:" class="choices" id="choice_2">Use Magic!</a>
    </div>

    <script type="text/javascript">
    var choice_1_1 = 'Slay the dragon using a red sword!';
    var choice_1_2 = 'Use magic to slay that evil beast!';
    var choice_1_text = 'The dragon attempts to eat you.';
    var choice_1_1_text = 'The dragon gives you burgers!';
    var choice_1_2_text = 'You turn into a cheeseburger.';
    var choice_2_1 = 'Make more delicious cheeseburgers.';
    var choice_2_2 = 'Sadly perish as if a cheeseburger.';
    var choice_2_text = 'The magic creates cheeseburgers.';
    var choice_2_1_text = 'The cheeseburgers taste fine!';
    var choice_2_2_text = 'The cheeseburgers eat you up!';
    function show_text(num) {
      var mytext = eval('choice'+num+'_text');
      $('text').set('text',mytext);
    }
    function set_links(num) {

      // create the first new A tag
      for(var both=1; both<3; both++) {
        //alert(mytext+"nnreplacing: choice"+num);
        var mytext = eval('choice'+num+'_'+both);

        // this is the sexy part where we create the A tag
        var new_a_tag = new Element('a',{
          'id': 'choice'+num+'_'+both,
          'href': 'javascript:',
          'text': mytext,
          'class': 'choices'
        }).replaces($('choice_'+both));

        // the new links need click events
        add_events(0);
      }
    }
    function add_events(set_the_links) {
      $$('.choices').addEvent('click', function() {
        var num = this.get('id').replace('choice','');
        show_text(num);
        if (set_the_links) set_links(num);
        else $$('.choices').destroy();
      });
    }
    add_events(1);
    </script>
```

How it works...

Creating an A tag element is very easy using MooTools' super-simple syntax. Seeing the semantics scripted sets the simplicity. The constructor syntax `new Element` declares a variable of class `Element`. The first argument of the class is the HTML tag, so we define an anchor tag by setting the letter A, lowercase, `a` as the first argument. Passing the HREF attribute and other properties is handled in the object hash passed in to the second, optional argument. The text to be linked is the property `text`, visible in the example.

There's more...

In the previous recipe we used `replaces()` on our newly formed element. We make use of that same replacement method to introduce our new element into the DOM.

The raw JavaScript built-in function `eval()` allows us to execute code for purposes such as dynamic variables. This recipe requires a method of concatenating variable names. Look in this example at how we loop over the choices `choice_1` and `choice_2` by concatenating their ID attributes: `$('choice_'+both)`. The variable `both` is defined and looped over in the `for()` loop above.

It is also important to be careful with how we use `eval()`. If unclean input is evaluated, it can open our code to script injection or simply make our code more difficult to read.

See also

The documentation is always a great place to spend time. Read about the `Element.replaces()` method on the official site: `http://mootools.net/docs/core/Element/Element#Element:replaces`.

Creating an IFRAME that displays google.com

Getting ready

In preparation for this one, some back-story is warranted. One useful tag in the HTML specification was not always supported by all major browsers, the IFRAME. The tag is now supported by all major browsers.

How to do it...

Use the SRC attribute to set the external or internal page to be displayed within this specified division of the page.

```
<form action="javascript:" method="get">
  <input id="submit" type="button" value="i can has search?"/>
</form>

<noscript>JavaScript is disabled.</noscript>
<script type="text/javascript">
$('submit').addEvent('click', function() {

    // use mootools to create an iframe element
    new Element('iframe', {
        'src'        : 'http://google.com',
        'frameborder': 1,
        'width'      : 800,
        'height'     : 400
    }).replaces($('submit'));

});
</script>
```

How it works...

In creating our IFRAME via MooTools, we make use of the class **Element**, feeding it the IFRAME tag as the first argument and the key/value properties to assign to the tag in the second.

There's more...

Later recipes deal with using asynchronous calls that likely preclude the necessity for using IFRAMEs in our applications. We will find there are valid applications of this tag; still, strive to use Ajax to replace on-page content and avoid some of the once-was feel of the IFRAME.

Injecting a "TD" data cell into a "TR" table row

One great use of asynchronous calls is to update tabular data. **This example bypasses the external request for data** and uses data statically defined so that we may concentrate on the injection of the TD data cell into an on-page data row.

Plan out on paper or in your mind's eye just what data will be changing. Even mocking up an example layout of the page, post-change, can really help us to write code that is more succinct, and does exactly what we need it to without passing through intermediate steps.

How to do it...

Create an initial table in which we can inject new information. Store in client-side code, static data that can be looped over and injected into the table upon each click of a button.

```html
<h1>World's Coolest Superheroes<h1>

<table border="1">
  <tr id="marble">
    <td>Spider-Man</td>
    <td>Iron Man</td>
    <td>Hulk</td>
  </tr>
</table>

<form action="javascript:" method="get">
  <input id="submit" type="button" value="Add a TD"/>
</form>

<script type="text/javascript">
  var other_heroes = ['Captain America', 'Daredevil', 'Wolverine',
    'Squirrel Girl'];
  var next = 0;
  var total = other_heroes.length;
  $('submit').addEvent('click', function() { add_hero(); });
  function add_hero() {

    // create a table cell (td) element
    var new_hero = new Element('td', {
      'display': 'inline-cell',
      'text': other_heroes[next]
    });
```

```
      // inject the td into the table row
      new_hero.inject('marble');

      next++;
      if (next>=total) $('submit').destroy();
   }
</script>
```

How it works...

The raw JavaScript-created array `other_heroes` provides the static data that we will add to our TR, `marble`. When the listener bound to `submit` is fired via the click action, our `add_hero()` function attempts to add a member of `other_heroes` to `marble`. Of course, once our static data pool is expended, we use `Element.destroy()` to remove the button from the DOM.

There's more...

While quite familiar with the two main style values for the property `display`, many hours of development have been wasted over the misunderstanding of the HTML specification behind how table elements are to be displayed. Find complete documentation on this subject at `http://www.w3.org/TR/CSS2/tables.html#value-def-table`.

The `display` style property values are:

▶ display: inline

▶ display: block

▶ display: table

▶ display: table-row

▶ display: table-cell

See also

Setting an incorrect display value will have very odd results across each major/minor browser. Not setting the value should produce the default and expected appearance; however, this may not be the case, *especially* with table elements in Internet Explorer. We can review the W3CSchools tutorial on display here: `http://www.w3schools.com/css/pr_class_display.asp`.

Injecting a "TR" data row into a "Table"

Those coming from the previous recipe will note quite a similarity. There are only a few differences in this example, and it shows how to handle rows instead of cells.

How to do it...

Inject a TR instead of a TD. Set the property HTML instead of TEXT in the `Element()` constructor, and the DOM markup will vary in that the table will expand vertically, via TR elements instead of horizontally via TD elements.

```
<h1>World's Coolest Superheroes </h1>

<form action="javascript:" method="get">
  <input id="submit" type="button" value="Add a TR"/>
</form>

<table border="1" id="marble">
  <tr>
    <th>Superhero</th>
  </tr>
</table>

<script type="text/javascript">
  var other_heroes = ['Spider-Man', 'Iron Man', 'Hulk',
    'Captain America', 'Daredevil', 'Wolverine', 'Squirrel Girl'];
  var next = 0;
  var total = other_heroes.length;
  $('submit').addEvent('click', add_hero);
  function add_hero() {

    // create a table row (tr) element
    var new_hero = new Element('tr', {
      'display': 'table-row',
      'html': '<td>'+other_heroes[next]+'</td>'
    });

    // inject the tr into the table row
    new_hero.inject('marble');

    next++;
    if (next>=total) $('submit').destroy();
  }
</script>
```

Each time we inject a new row, the table grows:

How it works...

Creating an HTML element is quite easy. Use the syntax `new Element('tr',{'html':'<td>hello world</td>'});` to create a TR element with the HTML property of a TD that has the text *hello world*. Injecting the row is simple using the `inject()` method that takes one mandatory and one optional argument. The first, mandatory argument is the ID attribute of the existing DOM element where the new element should be injected. The second, optional element indicates whether the element should be injected `before`, `after`, `top`, or the default value `bottom`.

There's more...

Knowing whether to inject *before*, *after*, *top*, or *bottom* may require a mind shift. Review this diagram to help us envision the options. If injecting an element *before* `my_element` then the first arrow indicates where in the DOM the injected element will go. Top goes inside and as the first element, as indicated by the second arrow. Bottom is also inside the referenced element, yet the injected element will be the last child of `my_element` (the reference element). And injecting the new element *after* the reference element positions the injected element next in the DOM as indicated by the fourth arrow.

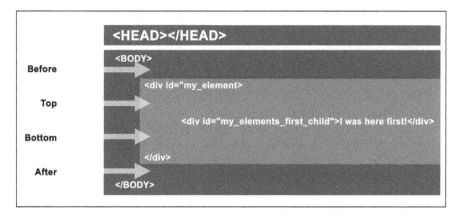

Injecting a table into the HTML DOM

Tuning in from the previous two recipes? Great! The superhero saga is about to be *tabled*, and you are just in time for today's exciting episode where we really get loopy on our heros!

How to do it...

We will create a table in memory and for each hero, build a `tr` with a `td` in it and finally inject the HTML table into the DOM.

```
<h1>World's Coolest Superheroes</h1>
</div>

    <form action="javascript:" method="get" id="my_form">
      <input id="submit" type="button" value="Add a TABLE"/>
    </form>

    <script type="text/javascript">
      var other_heroes = ['Spider-Man', 'Iron Man', 'Hulk',
        'Captain America', 'Daredevil', 'Wolverine', 'Squirrel Girl'];
      var next = 0;
      var total = other_heroes.length;
      $('submit').addEvent('click', function() { add_hero_table(); });
      function add_hero_table() {

        // create a new table element
        var my_hero_table = new Element('table',{ 'border':1 });

        // for each hero, build a tr with a td in it for each hero
        other_heroes.forEach(function(hero) {
```

```
        // inject, via grab(), each new tr element
        my_hero_table.grab(add_hero(hero));
    });
    // introduce the table to the dom by replacing the form
    my_hero_table.replaces('my_form');
}
function add_hero(hero) {
    // create a table row (td) element
    var new_hero = new Element('td', {'text':hero});
    // create a table row (tr) element to hold the td element
    var new_hero_row = new Element('tr');
    // inject our td into our tr
    new_hero_row.grab(new_hero);
    // send it to the requestor
    return new_hero_row;
}
</script>
```

How it works...

The function that we have been using, `add_hero()`, is re-purposed to create TDs and TRs individually, each via the `Element()` constructor. We still loop over each element of our hero array, but only after we use the constructor to create a TABLE element into which each TR element (itself containing each TD element) will be injected.

There's more...

The `Element.grab()` injection method reverses the usage of `Element.inject()` causing the firing element to be reversed with the target element, syntactically speaking. Many find it easier to read than `inject()`, and there is no overhead from using it one way or the other.

If we need to pass before or after, we must use `inject()` as only *top* and *bottom* are acceptable second arguments for `grab()`.

Creating an "A" tag link that alters the src of an IFRAME

Imagine how our alarm clock works. We set a *listener*, so to speak, on the device such that it *listens* and waits for the action of the time we wish to receive an alarm. In our HTML DOM, we can add listening events as properties when we create an element. When the listener is fired, the defined action will execute!

How to do it...

Create an anchor tag, set a listener on it, and define the action to take when the listener is activated, in other words, do something when the link is clicked:

```
<iframe id="miframe" src="http://bing.com" width="800" height="400"></
iframe>

<style type="text/css">
a { cursor:pointer; display:block; color:#00F;
  text-decoration:underline; font-size:20px; }
</style>

<noscript>JavaScript is disabled.</noscript>
<script type="text/javascript">

// create an a tag to add to the dom
var bung = new Element('a',{
  'text': 'Google, please.'
});

// put a listener on our a tag
bung.addEvent('click',function() {
  // change the iframe src to google
  $('miframe').set('src','http://google.com');
  this.destroy();
});

// inject our a tag into the dom
bung.inject('miframe','before');
</script>
```

How it works...

In this example, an existing IFRAME is displaying a search engine via the `src` attribute `http://bing.com`. Our DOM injected A tag simply has the text **Google, please.**. Before injecting this tag into the DOM, we use the `addEvent()` method of that element to create an anonymous function that sets the `src` property of `miframe`, the existing IFRAME already in the DOM. To prevent the useless clicking of a one-time, disposable user interface widget, we then destroy the A tag, `this.destroy()`.

There's more...

Covered frequently in this chapter, `Element.inject()` takes two arguments that tell which element is the location identifier of where to add the element into the DOM and, respectively, where to add the element *in relation to* that identifier.

See also

The MooTorial.com website is a great reference for documentation and examples on everything Moo, including `Element.inject()`:
`http://mootorial.com/wiki/mootorial/04-element/00-element#element.inject`.

Creating a DIV displaying an Ajax form response

The creation of new DOM elements with MooTools is elementary, as is calling asynchronous JavaScript requests, Ajax. Here we combine the two for a very reusable recipe where the results of a form submission are displayed on the same page as the request. Hook the Ajax call up to your server-side script and make *form magic.* To avoid the necessity of server-side scripting, we call our own HTML markup and display that in this example.

How to do it...

```
<form action="javascript:" method="get">
  <input type="button" id="mybutton" value="Ajax and Response!"
    onclick="ajax_it();"/>
</form>
<span id="put_it_here">Waiting for form submission...</span>

<script type="text/javascript">

// A
// make a new ajax request
var myJax = new Request({
  // A1
  url: '?',
  // A2
  onSuccess: function(response) {

    // if the ajax is called twice, empty the div
    $('put_it_here').empty();
```

```
    // B
    // make a new DOM element
    var myDiv = new Element('div', {
       'id': 'put_it_here',
       'text': 'Thanks, we processed the form and here is the
          result: '+response
    }).replaces('put_it_here');


    }
});
function ajax_it() {
   myJax.send();
}
</script>
```

How it works...

Note that our action simply calls the current page, thusly displaying the contents of the HTML source:

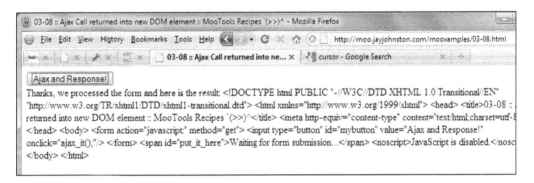

There are two pieces of pertinent code here. The first, *A* is where the Ajax request is created and defined. To specify the URL, look to the recipe line denoted, *A1*. In this version of the recipe, we call our own page by sending an empty query string, ?. Change this academic example into a working application by replacing ? with a server-side script. It may look something like `process_my_ajax.cfm` or `process_my_ajax.php`.

The second notable instantiation, the DOM element addition, is nested within the `onSuccess()` method of `myJax`. In *B*, we redefine the ID attribute, again to `put_it_here` so that we can call the Ajax multiple times; and we place the response of the asynchronous JavaScript call into the text of the element.

Server-side scripting is a staple when it comes to asynchronous scripting. When we are familiar with PHP or ColdFusion, then we know right away that the `url` property of our Ajax request will need to have a `.php` or `.cfm` extension. Learn more about the freely downloadable PHP at `http://php.net` or go to Adobe's website, `http://www.adobe.com/products/coldfusion/` to learn about ColdFusion. Those two server-side scripting languages are popular, but the gamut of server-side scripting languages is difficult to fathom and truly impossible to list entirely in one place; well, at least impossible to list in the scope of this informational block.

There's more...

For an interesting effect with the code in this recipe, alter the `text` property declaration in `myDiv` to the property `html` instead, but *leave the value* to be the incoming `response` variable. Run this and see what happens; be sure to send the Ajax multiple times. The effect is much like standing between two mirrors. Crazy! At first glance, this may seem like a useless parlor trick; but in fact, using Ajax to call server-side scripts that inject HTML back into our DOM is exactly how high-powered applications like *Google Calendar* function so well.

Creating new form elements

Creating new form elements uses the same easy-to-remember syntax as creating any other HTML elements. We can then inject them into our form on the fly. Prepare by being familiar with this syntax.

How to do it...

Create new form elements that each have a unique name.

```
<form action="javascript:" method="get" id="my_form">
  <input type="button" id="add_input" value="Add Input"/>
  <input type="button" id="my_submit" value="Submit Form"/>
</form>

<script type="text/javascript">
var num_els = 0;
$('add_input').addEvent('click',function() {
  num_els++;

  // create a new FORM element (INPUT)
  new Element('input',{
```

```
        'type' : 'text',
        'name' : 'input_'+num_els,
        'value': String.uniqueID(),
        'style': 'display:block;'
      }).inject('my_form','bottom');

  });
  $('my_submit').addEvent('click',function() {
    $$('#my_form input[type=text]').forEach(function(el) {
      var my_name  = el.get('name');
      var my_value = el.get('value');
      alert('Input Named "'+my_name+'" has value "'+my_value+'"');
    });
  });
  </script>
</body>
</html>
```

How it works...

The form in this example begins with just two input elements that are of `type="button"`, so no data would be transferred should this form be submitted. In order to add items that will transfer client data, we attach an event listener to the button labeled "Add Input". Each time this button is clicked, a bound function creates a new `INPUT` element. The syntax is the same for creating form elements as for other HTML elements: the first argument is the HTML tag, `input`, and the second argument is a hash object of the properties to define in the tag.

In this recipe, each new `INPUT` element added is created with an incrementing name that includes the string, "input_" concatenated with the current value of `num_els`. Increasing `num_els` with each click of `add_input` allows us to get a unique input `name` attribute for each element. To once again demonstrate the use of `String.uniqueID()`, as demonstrated in *Chapter 2, Switching Paddles Midstream: Changing HTML after Page Load*, we define the value of each element with a unique string generated off the base of a current timestamp.

There's more...

The `action` attribute of a `FORM` tag is mandatory. Even if our form will not be used to submit via HTTP refresh (page reload) we must include it.

The `action` **attribute of** FORM

The `action="javascript:"` found in our recipes indicates that no action other than JavaScript should be taken when the form is submitted. Change the `action` attribute from `javascript:` to the fully qualified, absolute, or relative path of the server-side script that will process the form.

To give the example some descriptive meaning and action, the "Submit Form" button is bound to a function that calls a loop over a group of elements made up by the CSS selector `#my_form input [type=text]`. Using the `Element.get()` method, we are able to alert the `name` and `value` of each element created by the `add_input`, click event.

Creating new form elements when more inputs are needed

Variable numbers of inputs can be tricky when creating a web form. We have all come across those web forms that have a static number of multiple blanks all set to take variable amounts of the same type of information. For instance, what if our form is to collect employment information; the arbitrary number of 5 blanks might be too many for some and still not enough for most. Creating that form with a **variable number of blanks** would solve that issue.

Getting ready

Knowing which information we need to collect will really speed up our development. We can write down on a sheet of paper the fields we will need to collect, group them intelligently, and then lay them out in our HTML in an eye-appealing fashion before beginning our JavaScript.

Before beginning the scripting, create a FORM that can be used in our recipe.

```
<form action="javascript:" method="get" id="my_form">
  <div id="my_parent">
  <div id="automobile1" style="background-color:#CDCDCD;
    margin:5px;">

  <table>
    <tr>
      <td style="width:300px;" valign="top"><p>
        <span class="x"></span> Automobile </p></td>
      <td valign="top"> </td>
    </tr>
    <tr>
      <td valign="top">Year,Make,Model</td>
```

```
          <td valign="top">
            <input name=yearmakemodel[]" title="Automobile Year,
              Make and Model" value="" type="text">
          </td>
        </tr>
        <tr>
          <td valign="top">Loan, Lease or Own</td>
          <td valign="top">
            <input name=loanlease[]" type="radio" class="rad2"
              value="loan"/>Loan<br />

            <input name=loanlease[]" type="radio" class="rad2"
              value="lease"/>Lease<br />
            <input name=loanlease[]" type="radio" class="rad2"
              value="own"/>Own
          </td>
        </tr>
        <tr>
          <td valign="top">Comprehensive</td>
          <td valign="top"><select name="coverageamount[]">
            <option value="$50000">$50,000</option>

            <option value="$100000">$100,000</option>
            <option value="$250000">$250,000</option>
            <option value="$500000">$500,000</option>
            <option value="$1000000">$1,000,000</option>
            <option value="$1500000">$1,500,000</option>
          </select></td>

        </tr>
        <tr><td colspan="2" align="right" valign="top"
          class="formspacer">
          <a href="javascript:newautomobile();">Add New Automobile</a>
          <span class="removeautomobile" style="display:none;">
          <a class="remove" id="1" style="cursor:pointer;">
          Remove this Automobile</a></span></td></tr>

      </table>
      <br/>
      </div>
      </div>
      <input type="button" id="my_submit" value="Submit Form"/>

</form>
```

How to do it...

Code the variable group of elements to have a trigger that creates new instances of that variable group of elements:

```
<script type="text/javascript">
function removeautomobile(el) {
  if (el!=='automobile1') {
    $(el).destroy();
  } else {
    // there is not an html widget to get here...hopefully
    alert('sorry, automobile #1 cannot be removed');
  }
}

var x = 1;
function newautomobile() {

  // do the clone
  var automobilediv = $('automobile1').clone();

  // variables we will need throughout
  v = x;
  x++;

  // the main div of each automobile must be named uniquely
  automobilediv.set('id','automobile'+x);

  // empty all the fields before injection
  var my_flds = automobilediv.getElements('input[type=text]');
  my_flds.set('value','');
  my_flds.value = '';

  // select elements empty differently
  var my_selects = automobilediv.getElements('select');
  my_selects.forEach(function(sel) { sel.selectedIndex = 0; });

  // before injection, update the radio button names
  var my_rad2 = automobilediv.getElements('input.rad2');
  var newradname = 'loanlease'+x;
  my_rad2.set('name',newradname);
  // radio button fields empty differently
  my_rad2.removeProperty('checked');
```

```
    // this is the magic
    automobilediv.inject('my_parent','top');

    // users appreciate landmarks
    $$('#automobile'+x+' .x').set('text','Additional ');
    $$('#automobile'+x+' .remove').each(function(item) {
      item.setStyle('cursor','pointer');
      item.set('id',x);
      item.addEvent('click',function() {
        var myid = this.get('id');
        removeautomobile('automobile'+myid);
      });
    });
    $$('#automobile'+x+' .removeautomobile').
      setStyle('display','inline');
}

</script>
```

How it works...

The dominoes set up to fall here are the form, the link to add a new form group, *Automobile*, and the code that duplicates the existing markup of that group. Once we have an HTML, syntax-compliant, initial markup, we attach a listener to our `Add Automobile` link, making it a trigger of the `newautomobile()` function.

The purpose of that function, `newautomobile()` is to copy the existing form by using `Element.clone()`. The work is not done, though, since we need to remove any existing values from the cloned element. Clearing values of `input[type=text]` elements is handled by setting the value to an empty string:

```
value=''
```

Some browsers require that both the raw JavaScript and the element property *value* are emptied. Save some cross browser frustration: set them both every time!

```
my_flds.set('value','');
my_flds.value = '';
```

Radio buttons require the `checked` property to be removed. Loop over each instance of a group of `RADIO` elements and uncheck each of them individually. Finally, be sure to set the `selectedIndex` of each `SELECT` element to zero to remove any selected value. If no value exists, then no error is thrown by this action.

Once the cloned script has all of its input widgets cleared of their values, we remember that there can be no duplication of ID attributes anywhere within the code block we are about to inject. Fortunately for us, we handled that early on within our cloning function: `automobilediv.set('id','automobile'+x);`.

Now inject into the top of `my_parent` and set the text of the group in such a way that the user recognizes the insertion of the new group. Injecting below elements is common, but the author has found that the *add, add, add* test-pattern implementation can confuse users since they do not realize the new elements are showing up outside the scrolled, viewable area.

There's more...

Be sure to code a removal button in case our users are born of the *double-click-even-though-the-link-is-a-single-click* variant of the population. Users invariably add more than they want to add, and especially, clients like to test this kind of form by repeatedly clicking *add, add, add* and then immediately complaining that they cannot get rid of the newly added element groups. This recipe carefully places a removal button on each of the newly created elements.

See also

At the time of writing, a similar example by the author is live at `http://bentonwhite.com/autoform.html`, with many other Moo-enhanced features as well. Be sure to pay close attention to the differences in that MooTools 1.1 version of this MooTools 1.3 recipe.

Adding a select box to the HTML DOM

Adding a `SELECT` box to the DOM can be tricky, but MooTools gives us the ability to make it look easy. This example will help us solve the common problem of a secondary `SELECT` menu upon modification of a first.

Getting ready

In our example, we ready ourselves by knowing the subordinate data to the first SELECT element's options. In a real-world usage, it is likely we would Ajax in the secondary data. If the planned use of the recipe includes Ajaxing in the secondary data, be sure to prepare the server-side script that returns the HTML before beginning.

How to do it...

Use a primary SELECT drop-down menu to dynamically create a secondary SELECT drop down:

```html
<form action="javascript:" method="get" id="my_form">
  <div id="automobile1" style="background-color:#CDCDCD;
    margin:5px;">
  <table>
    <tr>
      <td valign="top">Loan, Lease or Own</td>
      <td valign="top">
        <input name=loanlease[]" type="radio" class="rad2"
          value="loan"/>Loan<br />
        <input name=loanlease[]" type="radio" class="rad2"
          value="lease"/>Lease<br />
        <input name=loanlease[]" type="radio" class="rad2"
          value="own"/>Own
      </td>
    </tr>
    <tr>
      <td valign="top">Next, Please Choose:</td>
      <td valign="top" id="put_er_here"></td>
    </tr>
  </table>
  <br/>
  </div>
  </div>
</form>

<script type="text/javascript">
  var loan = '<option value="">Choose loan amount
    remaining:</option><option value="1">A Lot</option>
    <option value="2">About Half</option><option value="3">
    Not Much!</option>';
  var lease = '<option value="">Choose lease type:</option>
    <option value="1">Dealer ripped me off</option>
    <option value="2">Manufacturer rebates saved me</option>
    <option value="3">I make a lot of money so whatever</option>';
  var own = '<option value="">Choose ownership
    description:</option><option value="1">
    It's an Adam Sandler car</option><option value="2">
    The car rarely breaks down</option><option value="3">
    She's auto-show worthy and just had her oil changed!</option>';
```

```
// model the data that might come back via ajax in a real-world
   application
var my_pretend_ajax_data = {'loan':loan,'lease':lease,'own':own};

$$('.rad2').addEvent('click', function() {
  // if there is anything in put_er_here, dump it
  $('put_er_here').empty();
  // *this* represents the element which is firing
  var my_value = this.value;
  // here we would replace this line with real ajax
  var n0t_ajax = eval('my_pretend_ajax_data.'+my_value);

  // and the coup de grace:
  new Element('select', {
    'name': 'other_stuff',
    'id': 'other_stuff',
    'html': n0t_ajax
  }).inject('put_er_here');

  // set her selection
  $('other_stuff').selectedIndex = 0;
});
</script>
```

How it works...

onChange

There are some cross-browser kinks to onChange in SELECT elements. Some browsers will not fire onChange until the focus has changed. Get around this by putting in a 'fake' button to woo users into changing focus after selection, or just use RADIO buttons.

The first step is to create the trigger; Element.addEvent() is ever-faithful in binding elements to functions. Our function then in turn checks to be certain that any previously existing SELECT element that might have been added is now *gone* by calling the empty() method upon it. Now we are set to create our new SELECT element!

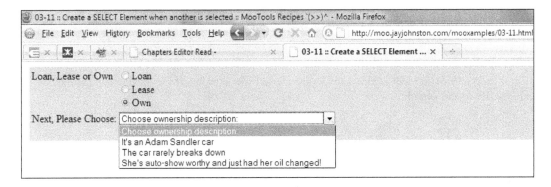

The syntax `new Element()` takes a first argument of the tag name. The second argument is a hash object of properties. Think over which properties we will need. If we do not add an ID attribute, we might not be able to later set the `selectedIndex` to auto-choose the option. And, of course, the `NAME` attribute is necessary for server-side processing after submission via HTTP refresh or via Ajax.

There's more...

The Ajax switcheroo here is so that we can focus on what is happening rather than where we are getting our HTML for the `SELECT` element. Here is an example of an Ajax call that would replace the line where `n0t_ajax` is defined.

```
// replace n0t_jax with Ajax
var myAjax = new Request.HTML({
  url : 'my_server_side_select_creator.php?my_value='+my_value,
  onSuccess : function(tree,elements,IS_ajax_html) {
    new Element('select', {
      'name': 'other_stuff', 'id': 'other_stuff', 'html':
        IS_ajax_html
    }).inject('put_er_here');
    $('other_stuff').selectedIndex = 0;
  }
}).get();
```

A complete version of the Ajax component and completed recipe can be seen in the files `my_server_side_select_creator.php` and `03-11b.html` of the code included with the book. We also use the Ajax component in the following recipe.

Adding a select option using Ajax

Often adding the entire select box is more than is needed to handle the job. Still using our previous recipe, let us just replace the option list of the existing SELECT element instead of adding the entire element.

Getting ready

This recipe is an extension of the previous recipe. Prepare for a simple twist that makes it easier to handle.

How to do it...

Create a FORM with a SELECT element. Use Ajax to call in new OPTION elements and inject them inside the SELECT element:

```
<form action="javascript:" method="get" id="my_form">
    <div id="automobile1" style="background-color:#CDCDCD;
      margin:5px;">
    <table>
      <tr>
        <td valign="top">Loan, Lease or Own</td>
        <td valign="top">
          <input name=loanlease[]" type="radio" class="rad2"
            value="loan"/>Loan<br />
          <input name=loanlease[]" type="radio" class="rad2"
            value="lease"/>Lease<br />
          <input name=loanlease[]" type="radio" class="rad2"
            value="own"/>Own
        </td>
      </tr>
      <tr>
        <td valign="top" colspan="2">
          <select name="next_choice" id="my_select_element">
            <option value=""><== Please choose Loan, Lease, or Own
              first</option>
          </select>
        </td>
      </tr>
    </table>
    <br/>
    </div>
    </div>
```

```
<script type="text/javascript">
  var loan = '<option value="">Choose loan amount
    remaining:</option><option value="1">A Lot</option>
    <option value="2">About Half</option>
    <option value="3">Not Much!</option>';
  var lease = '<option value="">Choose lease type:</option>
    <option value="1">Dealer ripped me off</option>
    <option value="2">Manufacturer rebates saved me</option>
    <option value="3">I make a lot of money so whatever</option>';
  var own = '<option value="">Choose ownership
    description:</option><option value="1">It's an Adam Sandler
    car</option><option value="2">The car rarely breaks
    down</option><option value="3">She's auto-show worthy and
    just had her oil changed!</option>';

  // model the data that might come back via ajax in a real-world
    application
  var my_pretend_ajax_data = {'loan':loan,'lease':lease,'own':own};

  $$('.rad2').addEvent('click', function() {
    var my_value = this.value;
    var myAjax = new Request.HTML({
      url : 'my_server_side_select_creator.php?my_value='+my_value,
      onSuccess : function(tree,elements,IS_ajax_html) {

        // it's easy to replace the innerHTML of an element
        $('my_select_element').set('html', IS_ajax_html).
          selectedIndex = 0;

      }
    }).get();
  })
</script>
```

How it works...

When we replace the **innerHTML** of an element, we save ourselves a few lines of code when compared to the process of injecting the entire element. We have also taken advantage of the ability for methods to be *chained* together. The code `selectedIndex = 0` is chained onto the `set()` action so that just after setting the HTML of `my_select_element`, the `selectedIndex` of the element is altered accordingly. Failing to set the `selectedIndex` may result in the automatic, unwanted selection of an OPTION in the SELECT element.

There's more...

When using Ajax to replace HTML, always be sure to validate the HTML of the end result. This can be hard do; however, when we use an initial, static markup to create our Ajax module, we can be sure that we have limited cross-browser issues to the best of our ability by using valid HTML markup.

See also

Later in the book we discuss some recipes and examples that will further our understanding of how chaining works.

4
That's Not All Folks: Animation and Scrolling

All animation used to be done with sequenced image formats, which were saved in **Graphics Interchange Format** (**GIF**). We all can remember cutesy, synchronized smiley faces, dolphins and bears, oh my! dancing around the text on our late '90s websites. Then came Flash which revolutionized animation by creating a language out of the sequencing methodology that could even enact external data source interaction.

Now we turn to Ajax to for our external data source interaction, allowing us to revisit the animation properties of JavaScript. Before we cringe with cutesy synchronization, revel in the knowledge that with the **MooTools Core as our abstraction layer** and *MooTools More as our animation layer*, animation has never been easier. And unlike Flash, we do not need high-powered licensing to code our next **User Interface** (**UI**).

- ▶ Scrolling elements, images, and text
- ▶ Grabbing attention with smoothly faded effects
- ▶ Creating mouse-overs, light-boxes, and ribbons

Scrolling a news box automatically

In this age of RSS and Twitter feed mania, we are frequently called upon as developers to create elements that can simply incorporate a complexity of data. Scrolling has proven to be a great way to do that since more data than can be displayed at once is still readily available.

Getting ready

Get ready to scroll some text or news by having a lot of text or news: at least more than what would fit within the defined element size.

Please also note that some long blocks of text are represented by ellipses in this and other recipes. They are removed here for display purposes, but necessary in the full example as shown in the code snippets attached with the book.

How to do it...

It is perfectly fine to Ajax-feed content into a DIV and then enact this scrolling effect upon it. Be sure that the Ajax has completed before calling the `Fx.Scroll()` class, since the instantiation will grab the height of the element, so changing it afterward could have undesirable *effects*.

```html
<script type="text/javascript" src="mootools-1.3.0.js"></script>
  <script type="text/javascript"
    src="mootools-more-1.3.0.js"></script>
</head>
<body>

    <div  id="news_outer">
        <div  id="news_inner">
Lorem  ipsum  dolor  sit  amet...<br/><br/>
        </div>
    </div>
    <style  type="text/css">
...
    </style>
    <noscript>JavaScript  is  disabled.</noscript>
    <script  type="text/javascript">
    var  characters  =  $('news_inner').get('html').length;
    var  milseconds  =  characters  *  50;

    var  my_news_scroller  =
      new  Fx.Scroll('news_outer'
        ,{'duration':milseconds,
          'transition':Fx.Transitions.linear});

    my_news_scroller.set(0,0);
    my_news_scroller.toBottom();

    </script>
```

How it works...

It is exciting to use a class like this that needs little explanation. Begin the scrolling instantiation with `var my_news_scroller = new Fx.Scroll(` and pass it the first argument, which is the outer boundary of the scrolling element.

> The outer bounding element *must* have a style of `overflow:hidden` since this is the mechanism that allows the effects class to scroll the text by adjusting the margin-top of its contained, internal element.

The second argument to pass can be any of the options defined in the base, `Fx` class or those created especially for the `Scroll()` method.

In our option list, we have passed a number of milliseconds that we wish for the effect to take to complete. Bypassing this option will cause **the default number milliseconds, 500**, to very quickly, albeit smoothly, rush through the scroll in a blinding half-second.

There are methods to be called upon this scrolling effect instantiation, most notably `set()`, which takes the `X` or `Y` values to which the element should be scrolled. In our example, we cannot know ahead of time how long our Lorem Ipsum makes the DIV element, so we take advantage of `toBottom()` and let the DOM handle passing the height and x/y axis information to `Fx.Scroll.toBottom()`.

There's more...

Lorem Ipsum was a technique that printers of yore used to fill space when setting type. The website design industry has taken hold of this practice and often uses it when laying out designs for clients. It makes a nifty news feed since clients seem to always worry incessantly about the content when designers are begging them to focus on layout. Lorem some Ipsum today!

See also

The list of options that are available to the `Fx` class can be found in the MooTools **More** documentation available at `http://mootools.net/docs/core/Fx/Fx#Fx:constructor`. Knowing those well will help us out extensively during the recipes of this chapter.

Showing a tall page slowly as visitors watch

With what we've seen in the previous recipe, you should understand that the methodology behind scrolling an element is based on a two-element structure where one is the smaller, viewable area that masks the larger, content-containing element, and this larger, content element scrolls smoothly behind the viewable element.

How to do it...

Create a DIV with some content in it that can be scrolled. Use Moo-effects to create the scrolling process, then listen for user input to adjust the scrolling mechanism.

```
<script  type="text/javascript"
  src="mootools-1.3.0.js"></script>
<script  type="text/javascript"
  src="mootools-more-1.3.0.js"></script>
</head>
<body>
    <div  id="news">
Lorem  ipsum  dolor  sit  amet,  ....<br/><br/>
    </div>
    <style  type="text/css">
...
    </style>
    <noscript>JavaScript  is  disabled.</noscript>
    <script  type="text/javascript">

    // create  the  container  to  scroll
    var  scrolling_body  =
      new  Fx.Scroll($$('body')[0],
        {'duration':30000,'transition':Fx.Transitions.linear});

    // begin  the  scrolling  effect
    scrolling_body.toBottom();

    // be  sure  we  don't  ignore  user  input
    window.addEvents({
        'mousedown',function()  {  scrolling_body.cancel();  },
        'keydown',    function()  {  scrolling_body.cancel();  },
    });
    </script>
```

How it works...

The `Fx.Scroll()` method will accept as the first argument a string, which is the ID attribute of the viewable area, masking element. We can also pass an actual element either in raw JavaScript longhand, for instance `document.body`, or in *MooHand* like this: `$$('body')[0]`.

Double Dollar Arrays?

The double dollar $$() construct takes any CSS selector; in this recipe, we select all tags that match body. We can access individual elements in this collection by using an array index syntax like what's shown in this *pseudocode*: Array[index]. These collections are zero based, meaning that the first element is index zero.

The second argument of the scroll instantiation contains options allowed in either the base Fx class, such as duration or transition. There are also options specific to scroll().

There's more...

In these first examples we are actually misusing the class just a tiny bit. Scroll was probably meant in design to only scroll pages and elements quickly, though is works pretty well in slow motion. Be sure to try using this method to navigate a large page with navigation that scrolls the page internally by passing a transition value of, say, 1000 or using the default, 500. The scroll is amazingly fast and smooth on computers that have good video memory.

See also

Be sure to review the specific Fx.Scroll() documentation at http://mootools.net/docs/more/Fx/Fx.Scroll#Fx-Scroll. Also, to see how internal links can be quickly scrolled, stay tuned for the next recipe on scrolling, "cause...that ain't all!"

Making anchors scroll smoothly into view rather than jump instantly

Many websites have had to make a list of internal anchors that cause the page to jump down to a particular section. The "jump" of the page is a bit of magic that many users do not recognize as an on-page link. Use this eye-candy effect to clearly show that the on-page link is scrolling the page.

Getting ready

Do not get up, do not get coffee, do not blink. The next recipe does days' worth of JavaScript work **in one line!** *Get ready to* smoothly scroll to an internal page link.

How to do it...

Brace yourself...

```
    <script type="text/javascript" src="mootools-1.3.0.js"></script>
    <script type="text/javascript"
      src="mootools-more-1.3.0.js"></script>
</head>
<body>

    Scrolling, Internal Navigation:
    <a name="my_top"></a>
    <ul id="my_nav">
      <li><a href="#lorem_ipsum">Lorem ipsum</a></li>
      <li><a href="#that_is_all">That's all!</a></li>
    </ul>

    <div id="lorem_ipsum">
      <a name="lorem_ipsum"></a>
...

      <a href="#my_top">Back to Top</a>
    </div>

    <div id="that_is_all">
      <a name="that_is_all"></a>
...

      <a href="#my_top">Back to Top</a>
    </div>

    </div>
    <style type="text/css">
...

    </style>
    <noscript>JavaScript is disabled.</noscript>
    <script type="text/javascript">

    // it shouldn't be this easy, right?
    var mySmoothScroll = new Fx.SmoothScroll();

    </script>
</body>
</html>
```

How it works...

Here is a screenshot of how the page looks after smoothly scrolling to one of the links.

There's more...

OH! We wanted to know what the wizard *behind* the curtain is doing. Okay, internally, MooTools More sets the options **links** and **locations** using this snippet:

```
location = win.location.href.match(/^[^#]*/)[0]  +  '#',
   links = $$(this.options.links  ||  this.doc.links);
```

We can manually set those options by passing an object hash of options to argument one of `Fx.SmoothScroll()`. It is obviously much easier to let the page smooth scroll all internal links by default. In the internal works of those two lines, the smooth scrolling object then pairs the assigned locations and links through name and then binds a click event to each link that overrides the default browser action.

Welcome visitors with a message that fades in for effect

In this recipe, you will learn how to fade in a block of text using color. Often, using a fade-in of a block of color will help users to orient themselves to what portion of the page is asking for attention.

Getting ready

Choose some text that needs to appear, perhaps an error message. Also, have a color palette in mind so that the design factor will not slow down the coding effort.

How to do it...

We begin with a recipe quite similar to the pop-up error injection recipe in *Chapter 3, And on the 8th Day: Creating HTML Elements*. The twist is that we fade in the error gently to increase the professionalism of the user interface. Note that we do not need the MooTools MORE in this recipe, though it is necessary for most of this chapter.

```
      <script   type="text/javascript"
        src="mootools-1.3.0.js"></script>
  </head>
  <body>
      <form   action="javascript:"   method="get">
          <span   id="my_error"></span>
          <input   id="submit"   type="button"   value="Submit   Form"/>
      </form>
      <noscript>JavaScript   is   disabled.</noscript>
      <script   type="text/javascript">
      $('submit').addEvent('click',   function()   {
          //  note   especially   the   style   color:#FFF
          my_error   =   new   Element('div',   {
              'id':   'my_error',
              'text':   'Error!',
              'style':   'width:200px;   color:#FFF;'
          }).replaces($('my_error'));

          //  fade   in   the   error   text
          $('my_error').tween('color','#F00');

          //  remove   the   error   after   three   seconds
          setTimeout("$('my_error').set(
            {'text':'','style':''})",3000);
      });
      </script>
```

How it works...

The `Fx` class is used to extend Moo-elements with the `Element.tween()` method. Not having to instantiate an effects class for each element that we wish to tween is a huge coding time saver! This method takes two or three arguments: the style property that should be animated and then the value of the tween. If we specify only two arguments, the second is used as the final value and the current value is used as the beginning value.

There's more...

The syntax for specifying both start and end values is:

```
myElement.tween(property, startValue[, endValue])
```

So for instance, in our recipe, we could change the fade in the error text line to this: `$('my_error').tween('color','#000',#F00')` for a slightly different effect where the text immediately become black on white instead of white on white and then fades to red using the default **transition** of 500 milliseconds.

See more

The documentation on custom **Element** methods that use the `Fx` base class are found in the documentation on effects: `http://mootools.net/docs/core/Fx/Fx.Tween#Element`.

Removing an error message from the page with a fade effect

We are all experienced with *showing* an error, but what happens to that error once the user has read it and begun to move on with their life? Fade out the error, or any block of text using opacity to help users have a better understanding of what the application is asking them to do.

Getting ready

Prepare to use this recipe in an application by listing out the form validation elements. Knowing which collection of elements must be integer, or string, and so on, will help us to write form validation that is more reusable, since we can reuse code that is written upon groups of elements more easily than we can use individual element's form validation. Once we are ready to do that, we will be eager to see how appealing we can make our error message!

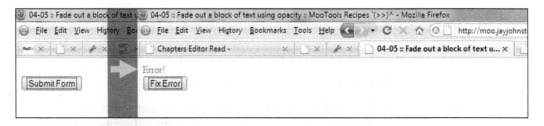

How to do it...

`Element.Fade()` helps us make an appealing message fade into place with utterly amazing simplicity. But do not stop there, be sure to have the message fade out with equal appeal!

```
        <script type="text/javascript"
          src="mootools-1.3.0.js"></script>
</head>
<body>
    <form action="javascript:" method="get">
        <div id="my_error" style="color:#F00;"> </div>
        <input id="submit" type="button" value="Submit Form"/>

    </form>
    <noscript>JavaScript is disabled.</noscript>
    <script type="text/javascript">
    // show an error
    $('submit').addEvent('click', function() {
        show_error();
    });
    function show_error() {
        $('my_error').fade('show');
        $('my_error').set('text','Error!');
        $('submit').set('value',
          'Fix Error').removeEvents().addEvent('click',
            function() {
```

```
                    remove_error_with_fade();
            });
    }
    function remove_error_with_fade()  {

            // remove  a  block  of  text  with  a  fade
            $('my_error').fade('out',  {'duration':'long'});

            $('submit').set('value',
               'Submit Form').removeEvents().addEvent('click',
                  function()  {
                     show_error();
            });
    }
    </script>
```

Code two named function blocks that handle the actions of removing and adding the error message. Then code the addition and removal of the listeners that call those named functions.

How it works...

The show_error() function:

- ▶ Fades in the error message without an animated transition using $('my_error').fade('show')
- ▶ Sets the error text to Error!
- ▶ And then chains three actions together on the submit button to set the button value, remove the existing bound function, and then add the new bound function

In remove_error_with_fade() we do the reverse and add a fading, animated transition to the process.

The fade() method is a custom type for the class Element. This means that we can use it on any MooTools-extended element: any element indicated by the dollar sign objects during definition. The first parameter of fade takes one of the following valid values: in, out, show, hide, toggle, or an opacity value between 0 and 1. Note in our recipe the demonstration of how show (and hide) bypass any animated transition. The second argument is consistent with other Fx derivative methods in that it takes an options hash object of allowed options.

There's more...

Toggle was added when MooTools took its *no-look-back leap* from version 1.1 to version 1.2. `Element.Toggle()` is a great way to show and hide elements with a faded transition without writing much code at all. Be sure to test the value of the opacity on the toggled element to determine the visibility or value of any sister elements that must toggle in sequence; some browsers may send rapid client input fast enough to get sister elements out of synchronization.

Welcoming visitors with a sliding message

Let's slide in text from off the page. Text that appears to slide in from the edge of the page no longer takes scads of digital x/y plot points and mathematical algorithms. The `Fx.Slide()` class takes care of those particulars and allows us to focus on a fancy presentation. All this goodness without excess overhead in the memory layer means a win-win situation for us and our clients...as well as a win for *their* clients, the end-line consumers of the work.

How to do it...

Choose some text and formatting to use before beginning. Mark up the page as if the block of text is already on the page. Choose the effects transition to use and fire off the effect with a slight delay so that users do not miss it.

```
<script  type="text/javascript"
  src="mootools-1.3.0.js"></script>
<!--  let's  n0t  forget  the  MORE  -->
<script  type="text/javascript"
  src="mootools-more-1.3.0.js"></script>

</head>
<body>

  <style  type="text/css">

  </style>
<div id="welcome_box">
  <div id="welcome">
    <h1>Welcome to Jombo.com!</h1>
      Everything is possible at jombocom!</div>
  </div>
</div>

<noscript>JavaScript is disabled.</noscript>
```

```
<script type="text/javascript">
var effects = new Fx.Slide('welcome', {
  duration: 2500,
  transition: Fx.Transitions.Bounce.easeOut
});
effects.hide('horizontal');

// wait a few seconds before sliding in the text
setTimeout("effects.slideIn('horizontal');",1000);

</script>
```

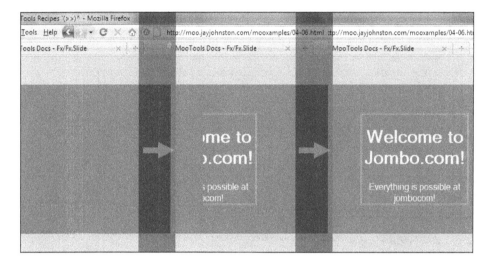

How it works...

The trick behind this beautiful idea is to use negative margins in the abstraction of Fx.Slide() to cause an element to appear to slide in from nowhere. We need not focus on that mysterious layer of magic, but simply pass the proper arguments to the constructor element new Fx.Slide() and then call the methods of the instantiation to enact the sliding animation.

Pass the constructor first, and most importantly, the ID attribute of the element that will be doing the movement. Note that objects that have advanced CSS positioning, such as ours with margin:auto, may need a parent container that is displayed with relative, block layout to contain them on our page. Once any optional hash object options of the Fx class are passed in to the second argument, our slide effect instantiation is complete.

Methods offered to our effects instantiation:

- ▶ `slideIn()`
- ▶ `slideOut()`
- ▶ `toggle()`
- ▶ `hide()`
- ▶ `show()`

To enact an automatic change in the visibility of the sliding effect element without using an animated transition, use `show()` and `hide()`.

There's more...

Sliding effects can be slid horizontally or vertically. Vertical sliding effects are the default; see in our recipe how we pass the text `horizontal` throughout the instantiations' method calls to our sliding effect.

We may not want an effect to take place right away, the raw JavaScript `setTimeout()` takes two arguments, the first being the function or script to execute and the second being the length in milliseconds to wait before executing the script.

See also

MooTools has an abstraction for `setTimeout` that will bind a named or anonymous function to a delay. Read about it at `http://mootools.net/docs/core/Types/Function#Function:delay`.

Also worth mention is the, slightly more wieldy, `Element.Slide()` custom type that will allow a very quick slide effect on any MooTooled element.

Creating an attention-grabber notification

In this recipe we will use background color and chain effects to bring a user's attention to some text.

Getting ready

Remember that flashing text can induce seizures. Think about the audience that will be using your application and keep flashing to a minimum. Use this effect in forms where changes in the DOM might be missed or mandatory form fields need to have the users' attention brought to them.

How to do it...

Use `Fx.Tween()` to animate a single CSS property.

```
<script  type="text/javascript"
  src="mootools-1.3.0.js"></script>
</head>
<body>
  <form  action="javascript:"  method="get">
      <input  id="submit" type="button"  value="Find  Lorem"/>

  </form>

  <div  id="lorem_ipsum">
      <h2  id="lorem_ipsum_h2">Lorem  ipsum</h2>
      Lorem ipsum dolor sit amet, consectetur adipiscing elit.
      <br/><br/>Donec eu sem velit, in cursus ligula.
      <br/><br/>Vestibulum commodo metus a ipsum ornare
          id faucibus metus sollicitudin.<br/><br/>
      <a  href="#my_top">Back  to  Top</a>
  </div>

  <noscript>JavaScript  is  disabled.</noscript>
  <script  type="text/javascript">
  // show  an  error
  $('submit').addEvent('click',  function()  {
      find_lorem();
  });
  function  find_lorem()  {

  // redundancy demonstrates Fx.Tween()s 1st arg flexibility
      var  my_element_2_animate  =  'lorem_ipsum_h2';
        // A
      var  my_element_2_animate  =  $$('#lorem_ipsum  h2')[0];
        // B

  // instantiate  the  Tween  class  object
      var lorem_tween  =
      new Fx.Tween(my_element_2_animate,
        {duration:100,link:'chain'});

  // choose some colors to loop through
        var  colors  =  ['#F33','#FF3','#FFF']
      colors.forEach(function(color)  {
```

```
        // chain up each color
        lorem_tween.start('background-color',color);

    });
}
</script>
```

As with all `Fx` classes, the first argument is the element to animate. In our second argument, the options hash, we are using the `link` option to pass the value "chain", which tells the instance of `tween` how to handle subsequent calls. Other valid values are "ignore", and "cancel".

Also different from our other recipes is the very short period we are using for the duration of the animation. Valid values are `"short"`, `"normal"`, `"long"` (250, 500, and 1000 milliseconds, respectively), along with any other integer representing the number of milliseconds to run the animation. As simple math will show, by chaining up three 100 millisecond tweens, we have created a 300 millisecond transition from white to red, red to yellow, and then yellow back to white in order to call our users' attention to the text.

There's more...

Now that we know the hard way to do it, try using `Element.highlight()`! Using this line, `my_element_2_animate.highlight()`, saves a lot of typing but loses some control over the exact animations performed. If doing something that begs for animation boldness, use the long method and switch from `Fx.Tween()` to `Fx.Morph()` so that multiple CSS properties can be morphed simultaneously. If just handling mandatory form elements, use the simpler `Element.highlight()`.

See also

This recipe did not use MooTools More! Be sure to read the differences in how MooTools Core and MooTools More use the `Fx` class.

- ▶ CORE: `http://mootools.net/docs/core/Fx/Fx#Fx`
- ▶ *MORE*: `http://mootools.net/docs/more/Fx/Fx.Elements`
- ▶ *MORE*: `http://mootools.net/docs/more/Fx/Fx.Accordion`
- ▶ *MORE*: `http://mootools.net/docs/more/Fx/Fx.Move`
- ▶ *MORE*: `http://mootools.net/docs/more/Fx/Fx.Reveal`
- ▶ *MORE*: `http://mootools.net/docs/more/Fx/Fx.Scroll`
- ▶ *MORE*: `http://mootools.net/docs/more/Fx/Fx.Slide`
- ▶ *MORE*: `http://mootools.net/docs/more/Fx/Fx.SmoothScroll`
- ▶ *MORE*: `http://mootools.net/docs/more/Fx/Fx.Sort`

Creating a scrolling thumbnail display

Often when we are putting together a web design, there is too much information or media to include in a single layer. Alter the design to reduce spatial requirements by making a line of thumbnails scroll automatically within a defined area. Scroll thumbnail images within a DIV.

How to do it...

On page-load, begin altering the margin of a DIV that is partially obscured with a style that hides overflow. Continue to alter the margin so that the DIV appears to slide or scroll gently to the left. When the DIV reaches its right-hand end, send it back in the other direction.

```html
<script  type="text/javascript"
  src="mootools-1.3.0.js"></script>
<!-- let's n0t forget the MORE -->
<script  type="text/javascript"
  src="mootools-more-1.3.0.js"></script>

</head>
<body>
  <div  id="pics_outer">
     <div  id="pics_inner">
          <img src="04-08_01.jpg"/>
          ...
          <img src="04-08_10.jpg"/>
     </div>
  </div>
  <style  type="text/css">
     #pics_outer  {
         /* required to make scroll work */
         overflow:  hidden;  width:600px;
```

```
        /* optional formatting */
        height:119px; border: 1px dotted #777;
          margin: 5px; padding: 5px;
      }
      #pics_inner {
          width:1520px; white-space: nowrap;
      }
    </style>

    <noscript>JavaScript is disabled.</noscript>
    <script type="text/javascript">
    var milliseconds = 10000;
    var direction = 'Right';
    var my_pics_scroller =
        new Fx.Scroll('pics_outer',
          {'duration':milliseconds,
            'transition':Fx.Transitions.linear});
    my_pics_scroller.addEvent('complete',function() {
        direction = (direction=='Right') ? 'Left' : 'Right';
        eval('my_pics_scroller.to'+direction+'();');
    });

    // in this case we *have* to wait until window load
    window.addEvent('load',function() {

        my_pics_scroller.set(0,0);
        my_pics_scroller.toRight();

    });
    </script>
```

How it works...

Using the effects class in MooTools More that animates scrolling is simple and only takes two arguments. The first, with which we are already familiar, is the string ID of the element to act upon. Remember when using Fx.Scroll(), the parent element must have overflow set to hidden in order to hide its overflow; that is a crucial step when using this class object! The second argument, an object hash, is optional and may be passed any number of Fx valid options, including the duration in milliseconds and the type of transition.

To be sure the page is not reloaded with a scroll that has halfway finished, first automatically reset the scrolling animation to its start position: my_pics_scroller.set(0,0). As we noted in the first recipe of this chapter, several handy methods like toRight() can be called upon the effects instantiation to effect movement.

There's more...

Several available events that are built into the `Fx` class allow us to further extend the functionality of the animation. In our recipe, we bind a function to the completion event *complete* that reverses the direction of the scrolling animation. After the animation completes a second time, the *complete* event is still bound and again reverses the direction of scrolling animation.

See also

There are many events and options available in the `Fx` class. Be sure to browse them before starting each project as they may have exactly the ticket to get us out of a tough programming spot with a client's difficult, 11th-hour request.

Launching a lightbox image from a thumbnail

When a thumbnail is clicked, let's launch a lightbox to show a larger version of the image.

Getting ready

We are working off the previous recipe; be sure to familiarize yourself with the concepts of the scrolling thumbnail list. Here we will add a pop-up-like lightbox overlay that will show a full version of any thumbnail image in our scrolling thumbnail display.

How to do it...

Continue the previous recipe and make it better by launching a lightbox on mouse-click. Style the lightbox such that the overlay uses a semi-transparent PNG image to partially obscure the background of the page.

```
<script  type="text/javascript"
  src="mootools-1.3.0.js"></script>
<!-- let's  n0t  forget  the  MORE  -->
<script  type="text/javascript"
  src="mootools-more-1.3.0.js"></script>

</head>
<body>
  <div  id="pics_outer">
      <div  id="pics_inner">
          <img src="04-08_01.jpg"/>
          ...
          <img src="04-08_10.jpg"/>
      </div>
  </div>
  <style  type="text/css">

  </style>

  <script  type="text/javascript">
  var  milliseconds  =  50000;
  var  direction  =  'Right';
  var  my_pics_scroller  =
    new  Fx.Scroll('pics_outer',
      {'duration':milliseconds,
        'transition':Fx.Transitions.linear});
  my_pics_scroller.addEvent('complete',function()  {
      direction  =  (direction=='Right')  ?  'Left'  :  'Right';
      eval('my_pics_scroller.to'+direction+'();');
  });

// in this case we *have* to wait until window load
  window.addEvent('load',function()  {
      my_pics_scroller.set(0,0);
      my_pics_scroller.toRight();
  });

// set up the listener for the images to launch the lightbox
  $$('#pics_inner  img').addEvent('click',function()  {
```

```
    // overlay page with lightbox transparency
    var lightbox = new Element('div',{
        'class': 'overlay lightbox',
        'opacity': .5,
    }).inject(document.body,'top');

// get the img src and inject it over the lightbox overlay
    var my_src = this.get('src');
    var img_full = my_src.replace('.jpg','_full.jpg');
    var my_html = '<tr><td><img
      src="'+img_full+'" alt=""/></td></tr>';

// overlay the overlay
    var lightpic = new Element('table',{
        'class': 'overlay lightpix',
        'html': my_html
    }).inject(document.body,'top').addEvent('click',
        function() { $$('.overlay').fade('out').destroy(); });
});

</script>
```

How it works...

Once we complete the scrolling thumbnail image display, we use the double dollar sign object ($$()), which takes a single string argument, a CSS selector string that *collects* all elements that match. The ten images that we have in DIV `pics_inner` are matched by the CSS selector `#pics_inner img`.

Agnostic as to which element has been clicked, our half-opaque overlay is created using the MooTools element constructor `Element()` to which we pass the element tag to create and the options hash object. The options passed for our overlay DIV set the classes `overlay` and `lightbox` as well as setting the opacity, which abstracts the various browser usages for transparency by allowing us to set a value from 0 to 1.

Now we must know which image was clicked so that we can open the proper thumbnail. Using the **this** keyword from within the scope created by the $$('#pics_inner img') collection loop allows us to quickly grab the *src* property: `this.get('src')`. The image naming schema expects each image to be named identically to the full image, save for the addition of _full just before the file ending. The raw JavaScript `replaces()` function replaces the first string argument with the second, thusly preparing for our script, in memory, the name of the full sized image.

Using CSS for layering that will place our image one layer higher than the half-opaque transparent lightbox layer, we create a table that will perfectly center our image both horizontally and vertically, which is embedded using the hash object property *html* during the MooTools element constructor call.

Both overlay class elements are injected into the top of the BODY, and the image layer itself, the highest layer based on its *z-index* style property, is bound through the *click* event to a function that removes both added overlay elements.

See also...

As alluded to in the *Getting ready* section, we will find more explanation on the scrolling thumbnail image portion of this recipe in the previous recipe.

Creating an application task ribbon that slides in

Ribbons are used these days to hold options for users; let's create a ribbon for our application.

Getting ready

The term *ribbon* is widely used to describe an area of an application or operating system that contains widgets, links, or other information. Look around your operating system for a ribbon to generate ideas on what you might add to a ribbon on your web application.

How to do it...

Not all ribbons have animation, but most do. Ours will slide in and out based on the mouse cursor entering and leaving the defined ribbon area.

```html
<script  type="text/javascript"
  src="mootools-1.3.0.js"></script>
<!-- let's n0t forget the MORE  -->
<script  type="text/javascript"
  src="mootools-more-1.3.0.js"></script>

</head>
<body>
    <div  id="ribbon_area">
    <div  id="ribbon">
        <a  href="http://twitter.com">
          <img  src="ribbon_01.jpg"
            alt="Twitter"  title="Twitter"/></a>
        <a  href="http://facebook.com">
          <img  src="ribbon_02.jpg"
            alt="Facebook"  title="Facebook"/></a>
        <a  href="http://linkedin.com">
          <img  src="ribbon_03.jpg"
            alt="LinkedIn"  title="LinkedIn"/></a>
        <a  href="http://google.com">
          <img  src="ribbon_06.jpg"
            alt="Google"  title="Google"/></a>
        <a  href="mailto:mooxamples_ribbon@jayjohnston.com">
          <img  src="ribbon_05.jpg"
            alt="Author's  Email"  title="Author's  Email"/></a>
    </div>
    </div>
    <style  type="text/css">
    body { background-color:#CCC; }
    #ribbon_area { position:fixed; top:0; left:0;
      height:72px; width:100%; z-index:999;
      background-color:transparent; }
    #ribbon { text-align:center;
      border-bottom:3px double #777; background-color:#FFF;
      width:100%; z-index:1000; }
    #ribbon a img { border:0; margin:2px 10px; }
    </style>
    <noscript>JavaScript is disabled.</noscript>
    <script type="text/javascript">

    // instantiate the slide effect
    var my_ribbon_slide = new Fx.Slide('ribbon');

    // hide the effect element
```

```
            my_ribbon_slide.hide();

            // call  the  events  to  slide  in  and  slide  out
            $('ribbon_area').addEvents({
                'mouseenter':function()  {
                    my_ribbon_slide.slideIn();
                },
                'mouseleave':function()  {
                    my_ribbon_slide.slideOut();
                }
            });
            </script>
```

Thanks to the extremely well developed MooTool More object, `Fx.Slide()`, the majority of the work we have to do in creating our ribbon is HTML markup. There must be a defined area that we can add events to so that our mouse-over and mouse-out actions will trigger the sliding effects, `<div id="ribbon_area">...</div>`. Then we fill that area with a DIV that will contain any widgets we place into our ribbon: `<div id="ribbon"></div>`. The ID attribute names chosen here are arbitrary and are not keywords.

Once the HTML and CSS create the two ribbon DIV items in a fashion that suits our website, we then need only instantiate the sliding effect object, `var my_ribbon_slide = new Fx.Slide('ribbon')`. The first argument of that object is the ID attribute of the element that we wish to slide in and out on our page. Valid methods that we can enact upon our instantiation include `slideIn()`, `slideOut()`, `toggle()`, `hide()`, and `show()`. These methods are self-explanatory, perhaps aside from the fact that *hide* and *show* have no animation but immediately set the position of the element, as in our recipe where we hide the element as the page is loading.

There's more...

In addition to the standard W3C events that can be passed to `addEvents()`, MooTools provides access to two custom events called `mouseenter` and `mouseleave`. There are instances when an element that is listening for mouse events also has children that are listening for mouse events. Use these two custom events to prevent the bubbling-up of events that unexpectedly cause multiple calls to mouse events in an unwanted manner.

See also

In a continuation of this recipe, the next recipe shows how to further enhance our ribbon by making the widgets grow towards the mouse!

Making mouseover elements grow on a ribbon

Ribbons often have a rollover effect; let's duplicate this effect for our ribbon.

Getting ready

Be sure to review the previous recipe as it goes through all the intricacies of the sliding task-bar ribbon used in this example.

How to do it...

What is new in this recipe begins with the comment *"// make the growth and shrinkage quick"*. There are three things that we have to accomplish, the first is placing listening events on the mouseover and mouseout. We use the MooTools custom events **mouseenter** and **mouseleave**, which help us avoid event bubbling.

...

```
<script  type="text/javascript">
//  ribbon  slide  in/slide  out  effects
```

...

```
//  make  the  growth  and  shrinkage  quick
$$('#ribbon  a  img').set('morph',{duration:'short'});

//  add  the  events  for  mouseover
$$('#ribbon  a  img').addEvents({
    'mouseenter':function()  {

        //  grows  the  hovered  image
        grow_shrink(this,64);

        //  grows  the  hovered  image's  previous  sibling
        if (this.getParent().getPrevious()) var to_my_left =
          this.getParent().getPrevious().getFirst('img');
        if (to_my_left) grow_shrink(to_my_left,48);

        //  grows  the  hovered  image's  next  sibling
        if (this.getParent().getNext()) var to_my_right =
          this.getParent().getNext().getFirst('img');
        if (to_my_right) grow_shrink(to_my_right,48);
```

```
        },
        'mouseleave':function() {

            // shrinks the hovered image and all siblings
            $$('#ribbon a img').each(function(el){
              grow_shrink(el,32);});


        }
    });

    function grow_shrink(el,size)  {
        el.morph({'width':size,'height':size});
    }

    </script>
```

How it works...

On mouse enter, we call the function `grow_shrink()`, which is set up to take the MooTool element object and size to which to morph the element, and morph them using the `Element.morph()` class. Since we are not passing a from-to object, morph knows to use the current height and width of the element and simply morph those current values to the ones passed in here. That simplifies the object-binding work we must do.

Finally, to add a smoothness to our roll-over effect, we code the immediate left and right siblings to grow to a size in between the 64 pixel mouse-over growth and the 32 pixel mouse-out, default size. Growing those siblings to 48 pixels is easy using our defined `grow_shrink()` function; however, getting just the right sibling to grow can be tricky.

There's more...

To tame the DOM and grab the elements that we need to grab, we could use a series of CSS selectors and compare that information with the ID attribute of our selected element. It is much easier, though, to turn to DOM hierarchy functions for this selection action.

 MooTools makes use of DOM hierarchy functions that help us grab elements relative to us.

Our recipe uses `Element.getParent()`, which grabs the parent element; in this case, it is the `<a href=""></a>` tag that surrounds the IMG tag represented by the `this` keyword. Also used, and fairly self-explanatory, are `Element.getPrevious()` and `Element.getNext()`, which grab the siblings immediately preceding and following our element. And finally, to get the first child element we implement `Element.getFirst()`.

See also

The MooTools documentation mixes the DOM functions for class `Element` with the other methods of that class. Reference that complete list at `http://mootools.net/docs/core/Element/Element`, and note the handy method list in the right-hand side column for quick navigation.

Making active elements on a ribbon bounce

Ribbons often have a bouncy effect for an active element; let's make our elements bounce.

Getting ready

The previous two recipes set up the hard work for this recipe where we simply add a bouncy effect to the roll-over images. Review those for more information on how to create a slide-in ribbon and links that grow and shrink with the mouse movement of the user.

How to do it...

Transitions are what make MooTools really far superior. Use them in this recipe to make the growth and shrinkage quick and make them bounce!

```
// make the growth and shrinkage quick
// and make them BOUNCE!
$$('#ribbon a img').set('morph',{
    duration:'long',
    // i can has mmm bop?
    transition:Fx.Transitions.Elastic.easeOut
});

// add the events for mouseover
$$('#ribbon a img').addEvents({
    'mouseenter':function()  {
        grow_shrink(this,64);
        if (this.getParent().getPrevious()) var to_my_left =
          this.getParent().getPrevious().getFirst('img');
        if (to_my_left) grow_shrink(to_my_left,48);
        if (this.getParent().getNext()) var to_my_right =
          this.getParent().getNext().getFirst('img');
        if (to_my_right) grow_shrink(to_my_right,48);
    },
    'mouseleave':function() {
        $$('#ribbon a img').each(function(el){
          grow_shrink(el,32);  });
    }
```

```
});
function  grow_shrink(el,size)  {
    el.morph({'width':size,'height':size});
}
```

How it works...

All `Fx` class derivatives can be passed a **transition**. Here, we pass `transition:`
`Fx.Transitions.Elastic.easeOut`, which instructs the algorithm for the growth and
shrinking we are doing in `Fx.Morph()`, instantiated through `Element.morph()` to first be
elastic, or stretch in nature. Then we cause the algorithm to slow its calculations towards the
end by using the keyword `easeOut`.

There's more...

Okay, the animation and scrolling of this chapter are just the mountain peak of a vast range of
mountainous terrain to soar across like an eagle! Let's go animate something!

5
Mr. Clean Uses Ajax: Remote Asynchronous Calls

Asynchronous JavaScript and XML, Ajax, is the primary tool of interactive web applications today. Interestingly, it is less of a tool and more of an idea. You see, the raw JavaScript *XMLHTTP Post* tools have been around for over a decade in the Mozilla/Safari form of `new XMLHttpRequest();` and the Internet Explorer form of `new ActiveXObject("Microsoft.XMLHTTP");`.

Once giants in the industry started using asynchronous requests to load data onto the page without a clunky HTTP refresh, it became industry standard and along with some transparency support in major browsers, helped to coin the somewhat dodgy term *Web 2.0*.

MooTools now brings us a cross-browser compliant method of implementing XMLHTTP Post operations without a lot of song and dance. In this chapter we will use the Ajax methods in the MooTool classes **Request** and **JSON** to accomplish:

- ▶ Displaying local and remote web pages and web page data
- ▶ Submitting forms and data and displaying their results
- ▶ Building widgets like a calculator, a stock ticker, and an MP3 list

Using Firefox's Firebug to troubleshoot asynchronous calls

The trickiest part of Ajax development is knowing what is happening in the seemingly *black box* request. Even if we define what data and URL we are using to make the request, if something happens that we have not accounted for in our coding, we may never know what was returned from the server.

Getting ready

Let us ready ourselves for this chapter by having one of the best tools to debug Ajax requests. We make ourselves familiar with Firefox Firebug, firstly, by downloading the Firefox browser from `http://firefox.com`. Once that is installed, we choose **Tools** from the horizontal menu, and then select **Add-ons** from the resulting drop-down menu. Finding and installing the Firebug add-on is simple; just search for Firebug and follow the directions to install it and restart Firefox. Once it is installed a tiny *firebug icon* will be evident in the status bar:

How to do it...

Clicking the icon once will open the *Firebug Window* (or press *F12*). Once the window is opened, choose the **Net** Panel from the list of Panels: **Console HTML CSS Script DOM Net**.

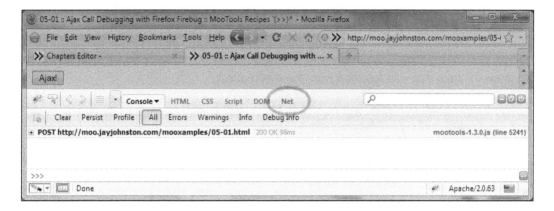

If the following message is visible in the **Net** Panel, **Net panel activated. Any requests while the net panel is inactive are not shown.**, simply refresh the page to activate the Net Panel in Firebug.

 Firebug is disabled by default in recent versions due to complaints that running it for every website causes overt memory usage.

How it works...

Now that Firebug Net Panel is open and accepting debugging information from our window, we use this code snippet to launch an Ajax request:

```html
<script type="text/javascript" src="mootools-1.3.0.js"></script>
</head>
<body>
  <form action="javascript:" method="get">
    <input type="button" id="mybutton" value="Ajax!"
      onclick="ajax_it();"/>
  </form>

  <script type="text/javascript">
  var myJax = new Request({
    url: '05-01.html'
  });
  function ajax_it() {
    myJax.send();
  }
  </script>
```

Look in Firebug Net Panel to see this request **POST 05-01.html**. It will follow several other requests, but it will be the one furthest down in the list. On a page with many requests, it will be necessary to scroll down to our Ajax request. Press the plus sign to expand the details of the request. Click the **Response** tab found just subordinate to the **POST 05-01.html** request to review the data that was returned from the Ajax request.

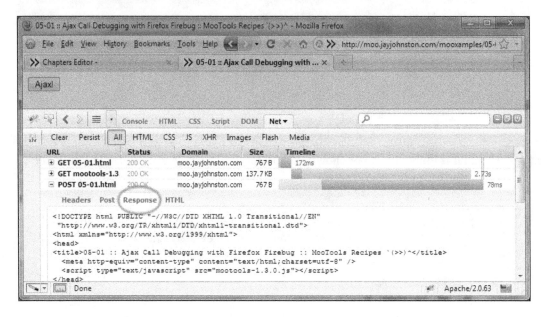

There's more...

Viewing the Ajax Response is not all we can do with Firebug Net Panel. We can also review the data that we posted, the headers of the request and the response, and any HTML that was returned with the response.

See also

As we maneuver through the Ajax examples in this chapter, we will keep our eyes on our Firebug Net Panels to be sure we are receiving the expected responses in each recipe. That will help keep our *server-side* errors from confusing our *client-side*, JavaScript, MooTool errors.

Displaying remote data via Ajax within a DIV

This recipe gets us ready for this chapter where Ajax is an idea of grabbing external data and bringing it into our current, already loaded page.

Getting ready

Prepare a small web page that is loaded with a static data "hello world". Name it
05_hello_world.html.

```html
<html>
<head><title>Display Local Data via Ajax Within A DIV</title></head>
<body>Hello World</body>
</html>
```

How to do it...

We will simply be loading this page via Ajax into the DOM on our page.

```html
<script type="text/javascript" src="mootools-1.3.0.js"></script>
</head>
<body>
  <form action="javascript:" method="get">
    <input type="button" id="mybutton" value="Ajax!"
      onclick="myJax.send();"/>
  </form>

  <fieldset style="padding:10px;"><legend>My Ajax Response:</legend>
    <div id="my_response"></div>
  </fieldset>

  <script type="text/javascript">
  var myJax = new Request({
    url: '05_hello_world.html',

    // fill the my_response DIV with the response html
    onSuccess: function(responseText, responseXML) {
      $('my_response').set('text',responseText);
    }

  });
  </script>
```

How it works...

MooTools abstracts the cross-browser issues with XMLHTTP Post actions, instantiating the proper browser-specific derivative to accomplish the task. We need only instantiate the `Request` class and then trigger `Request.send()` to fire the Ajax request.

Once the request completes successfully, the function bound to `onSuccess` receives the response text and response XML arguments and runs the code block we created. In this recipe the function makes use of `Element.set()` to set the inner text of the element to the value of `responseText`.

There's more...

Coding for every eventuality is tough business. We should, in every production application, code for the `onFailure` event. *On any given Sunday*, our user might lose their Internet connection and wonder for hours why the page does not seem to be doing anything.

See also

This simple example has us ready to graduate to the Intermediate Ajaxian level. Check out the next recipe where we handle cross-domain issues with Ajax using server-side code.

Displaying cross domain remote data via Ajax within a DIV

Ajax, inherently, cannot make a call to another domain. When we need to grab remote data from another domain, we have to turn to some kind of helper to get the data.

Getting ready

This example requires either PHP or ColdFusion to be installed on our development machine. The example shows a call to `05_remote_data.php`. If we are using ColdFusion, please use the included snippet named `05_remote_data.cfm` instead.

The recipe is a continuation of what we are working on in the previous, local data request recipe. When we are familiar with those concepts, adding the remote call will be an easy stepping stone.

How to do it...

Interestingly, the client-side portion of this only changes in the URL variable. We call the server-side script instead of the static, local data page.

```
<script type="text/javascript" src="mootools-1.3.0.js"></script>
</head>
<body>
  <form action="javascript:" method="get">
    <input type="button" id="mybutton" value="Ajax!"
      onclick="myJax.send();"/>
  </form>
  <fieldset style="padding:10px;"><legend>My Ajax Response:</legend>
    <div id="my_response"></div>
  </fieldset>

  <script type="text/javascript">
  var myJax = new Request({

    // remote calls will not work without some helper
    //url: 'http://webjuju.com/moo/05_remote_data.txt',

    // use server side code like php or coldfusion
    url: '05_remote_data.php',

    // fill the my_response DIV with the response html
    onSuccess: function(responseText, responseXML) {
      $('my_response').set('html',responseText);
    }
  });
  </script>
```

When the code completes, after pressing **Ajax!**, the user will see the **My Ajax Response** added to the DIV: **Hello (Remote) World**. In the event that we do not receive that message shortly after pressing the button, we can check the Firefox Firebug Net Panel to see the status of our request.

How it works...

If we remove the commenting slashes from "A" and run it instead of "B", we will find that *we are unable to grab the remote .txt* document. We must use server-side code or some other helper module to grab the remote data for us. In this recipe, we are using a simple PHP script that does not require PHP experience, if any, to grab the remote data and echo it back to our Ajax call locally.

Security mechanisms within raw JavaScript are at work here. MooTools itself is not preventing the remote calls, the underlying JavaScript architecture is attempting to keep our users safe from cross-site scripting, XSS, whereby ne'er-do-well sites use existing web cookies for a remote domain to gain evil access behind the scenes and unbeknown to the silently duped visitor.

There's more...

PHP is a good choice because it has a C-like syntax, wonderful documentation, and is free to download to virtually any platform. ColdFusion is good to use because an inexpensive ColdFusion, shared host can run as low as $2.95/month and the syntax is reminiscent of HTML markup. Of course, PHP and ColdFusion are not the only server-side languages. Many people like ASP.net, Ruby, or Java, among others, the list is endless and would leave me with a LISP if I tried to complete it.

See also

If you are curious about the PHP syntax used to grab the remote page, browse the documentation here: `http://php.net/file_get_contents`. Arguably, one of the best (fastest) resources for ColdFusion documentation is `http://cfquickdocs.com/cf8/`.

Screen scraping a portion of another web page

Grabbing data from another web page can either be illegal or a last ditch effort to overcome a data issue. The industry pet name for grabbing another web page and parsing out the needed data is called "Screen Scraping".

 Remember, screen scraping a website that we do not have permission to use the data from is illegal and can land us and our firm in a lot of unnecessary hot water!

Getting ready

All the legal mumbo-jumbo aside, screen scraping has many legal, and purposeful uses. To implement this recipe, imagine a scenario whereby the menu of one internal, company-owned website needs to be displayed within an area of another, separately maintained, company-owned website. Using a web service or other XML feed is one way to handle that; but experienced programmers know, we can typically scrape that data and redisplay it before the initial XML specifications can even be documented.

Screen Scraping 101

▶ Scrape only pages that we are licensed to scrape

▶ Scrape only pages that are not going to have HTML markup changes

▶ Scrape only when other, more documented methods like RSS are unavailable

▶ Content brought in via Ajax screen scraping will not be picked up by search engine robots

How to do it...

The United States Department of Commerce agency, National Institute of Standards and Technology, and U.S. Naval Observatory provide a free, public service with no usage limitations. Let us pull the central time zone, current atomic time, and display it on our page http://www.time.gov/timezone.cgi?Central/d/-6.

```
<script type="text/javascript" src="mootools-1.3.0.js"></script>
</head>
<body>
  The Centeral U.S. time at load (
    according to the U.S. Government atomic timeclocks):
  <h1 id="current_time"></h1>

  <script type="text/javascript">
  var myJax = new Request({

    // use server side code like php or coldfusion
    url: '05_scrape_time.gov.php',

    // fill the my_response DIV with the response html
    onSuccess: function(responseText) {
      // split the responseText (match our regex)
      var responseBody = responseText.substr(
        responseText.indexOf('<body'));
      // create a regex pattern to match the time
      var pattern = /([0-9]{1,2}:[0-9]{2}):[0-9]{2}/m;
      // find the time in the remaining reponse body
      var time = responseBody.match(pattern);
      // there may have been an error returned from the server
      var current_time = (!$defined(time)) ? responseText : time[1];
      // change the innerHTML of #current_time
```

```
        $('current_time').set('html',current_time);
    }
}).send();
</script>
```

To screen-scrape the current time from the cross-domain, remote website using Ajax, we must use a server-side script to grab the remote web page and then parse it to find the data we need. In our example, we use PHP (the ColdFusion example is included in the code snippets). Our Ajax request in MooTools, `var myJax = new Request(...).send();`, first makes an asynchronous XMLHTTP request to `url`, `05_scrape_time.gov.php`.

In the personified eyes of Mr. Clean, the Ajax process, this call to our *same domain script*, **is not a cross-domain call**. The cross-domain part happens within that script. PHP (or ColdFusion) makes a second asynchronous request while Ajax waits for the response from its initial call to the server-side script. Once the server-side script completes, the output from that script, in our case the body of `http://www.time.gov/timezone.cgi?Central/d/-6`, is returned and used by `Request.onSuccess()` as the `responseText`.

There's more...

Though our request object has now received the response from the server-side script that completed our cross-domain request, we have not yet whittled down the large return to the *time string* that is our data to display in the DIV, `current_time`. Making use of raw JavaScript, we create a simple regular expression, *regex pattern*, and pass that pattern to `String.match()` to find matches for that pattern.

More than one subpattern match is returned, so it is necessary for us to use the array indicator to access the part of the time string that we seek. Once that is accomplished, we use MooTools' `Element.set()` to set the `innerHTML`, `html`, of `current_time`.

See also

Learn more about the power of regex at W3Schools.com using these links:

- ▶ `http://www.w3schools.com/jsref/jsref_match.asp`
- ▶ `http://www.w3schools.com/jsref/jsref_obj_regexp.asp`

There is also a handy method in MooTools worth using to automatically escape the special characters in a regex pattern: `String.escapeRegExp()`.

Parsing and displaying JSON data

JavaScript Object Notation, JSON, is a simple way to provide complex data that can be passed like a scalar variable during the HTTP post process, which allows it to be passed quite easily.

How to do it...

Prepare a server-side script that will return a JSON object. In our example, we use a very simple JSON object that has one scalar variable containing the string "hello world".

```
<script type="text/javascript" src="mootools-1.3.0.js"></script>
</head>
<body>

  <form action="javascript:" method="get">
    <input type="button" id="mybutton" value="JSON!"
      onclick="myJax.send();"/>
  </form>
  <h1 id="json_greeting_div"></h1>

  <script type="text/javascript">

  // request is extended with the Request.JSON class
  var myJax = new Request.JSON({

    url: '05_json_data.txt',

    // the response argument is the json object
    onSuccess: function(json_response) {
      var json_greeting_var = json_response.greeting;
      $('json_greeting_div').set('html',json_greeting_var);

      $('mybutton').setStyle('visibility','hidden');
    }
  });
  </script>
```

How it works...

Much like the previous `Request()` examples, `Request.JSON()` is a class that is crafted for the transport of one particular type of cargo: JSON objects. The response argument sent to `Request.JSON.onSuccess()` is the JSON object. Parsing the object is terribly elementary and uses the dot notation to pick up properties of the object.

There's more...

In our example, there is no need to encode or decode JSON objects to or from strings; however, the **JSON** utility in MooTools allows us to move into or out of JSON encoded strings using `JSON.encode()` and `JSON.decode()`!

See also

When working with cross-domain remote data, we have seen that it is necessary to use server-side scripting to do the domain interaction. Review `http://mootools.net/docs/more/Request/Request.JSONP#Request-JSONP` to see how using *callbacks*, JavaScript will allow this cross-domain interaction. In short, a callback is posted with the request, and that external domain must respond with the proper callback response to verify security of the request.

In the next example, we will use JSON callbacks to receive a remote web service.

Parsing and displaying a web service

There are two kinds of web services, those that are easy to deal with and those that major in their ability to pain the derriere. Google's web services are among the easiest to work with. They come documented with clear, concise instructions and really useful examples that work out of the box.

How to do it...

Choose a web service. We are going to use Google's search API for this recipe. Be sure to look back in *Chapter 1, Oldies-but-Goodies: Foundational Moo* for information on getting a Google API key. The one we signed up for there will work fine for this example as well!

```
<script type="text/javascript" src="mootools-1.3.0.js"></script>
  <!-- let's n0t forget the MORE -->
  <script type="text/javascript" src="mootools-more-1.3.0.js"></
script>
</head>
```

We have not been including the MooTools More in this chapter, but it is necessary in this recipe since we are using **JSONP**.

```
<body>
  <form action="javascript:" method="get">
    Search for <input type="text" id="q" value="MooTools Jay
      Johnston Packt"/>
```

```
    <input type="button" id="mybutton" value="JSON Google Web
      Service!"
      onclick="

        myJax.send({
          data:{
            'q': $('q').value
          }

        });"/>
</form>
<div id="json_data"></div>

<script type="text/javascript">
<!-- do not forget to get your own google api code!  check back in
  recipe 01-03 for info! -->
var google_api_key = 'OUR-KEY-HERE';

// request is extended with the Request.JSON class
var myJax = new Request.JSONP({
  callbackKey: 'callback',
  // use the google api with our domain specific api key
  url: "https://ajax.googleapis.com/ajax/services
    /search/web?v=1.0&key="+google_api_key,

  // receive the response from google
  onComplete: function(google_json_response) {
    var search_results = google_json_response.responseData.results;

    // parse the data into html
    var stuff = '';
    search_results.each(function(el) {
      stuff += '<br/><a href="'+el.url+'">'+el.title+'</a>';
    });

    // introduce the html parsed from json into the dom
    $('json_data').set('html',stuff);

  }
});
</script>
```

How it works...

Setting up the variable `myJax` takes only a bit of the same work we have been doing with other MooTools **Request** derivative classes. This time we make use of `Request.JSONP()`, which automatically handles the cross-domain security of the *callback*, which is a simple mechanism that tells both domains that they are not being scammed by sharing a string value in the request and response.

We load our `JSONP.onComplete()` method with the parsing code that will pick up our JSON-encoded values, and loop over them to pick up the `url` and `title` properties that we need to build some HTML for our search response.

Take a look at the clever construction of the `onclick=""` attribute in our `INPUT` button, `mybutton`. That sends the JSON request. But it also does something much more important than that. The **JSONP** class allows for an option with key name **data** to be populated with an object of data to send. Google needs to know what we are searching for! The magic happens when we use the MooTool dollar object **$()** to grab the value of the element with ID attribute `mybutton`. This value is then passed in with the options that are the optional argument allowed with the method `JSONP.send()`. This sets the data that is sent along with the URL request to Google.

See also

In preparation for this recipe, the author reviewed publicly available JSON feeds and found this one, which is a great option for neophyte, JSON feed parsing: `http://search.usa.gov/api/recalls`. It has good documentation on the structure of the return and how to use the callback key.

Submitting a form using Ajax

We can really clean up a messy application by keeping forms and form requests together on one page.

Getting ready

Our form processor will need to be created before testing our Ajax. Included in the code snippets for the book are two processors that only echo the submitted values. These are meant for illustrative purposes and would need more server-side coding work to either submit the values to a database or to e-mail the values to a recipient.

How to do it...

Use the PHP form processor included in the book to echo values submitted via an Ajax form.

```
<script type="text/javascript" src="mootools-1.3.0.js"></script>
</head>
<body>
  <div id="error"></div>
  <form id="my_form" action="05_form_processor.php" method="post">
    Your name: <input type="text" name="name" value=""/><br/>
    Send an error? <input type="checkbox"
      name="error" value="1"/><br/>
    <input type="submit" value="Submit Form!"/>
  </form>

  <noscript>JavaScript is disabled.</noscript>
  <script type="text/javascript">

  $('my_form').set('send', {
    onComplete: function(response) {
      var error_test = response.substr(0,5);
      if (error_test.test('error','i')) {
        $('error').set('html',response);
      } else {
        $('my_form').set('html',response);
      }
    }
  });

  // bind a function to the submit event
  $('my_form').addEvent('submit',function(e) {

    // MooTools class and method to extend HTML events
    var event = new Event(e);
    e.stop();

    $('my_form').send();

  });
  </script>
```

How it works...

The syntax and process for submitting a form via Ajax are simple. We bind an action to the submit event of our form and use that to stop the HTML event. If JavaScript is disabled, the form will gracefully degrade the HTTP refresh to the processor normally!

We test for a key in the response to know whether or not there has been an error. If no error is found, then we remove the form and display the HTML results. If an error is found, then we display the error in the error DIV.

There's more...

Note how we use MooTools' `String.test` with the first argument being the needle to find in the string haystack and the second argument being a case insensitivity switch. Be sure to work closely with whomever is writing the form processor to be sure they are aware that errors in the form submission return that string properly as the first 5 characters.

See also

We bone up on our ability to manipulate strings at the MooTools documentation, `http://mootools.net/docs/core/Types/String#String:test`.

Building a calculator using Ajax

Included with the book are two versions of the calculator processor, the server-side script that processes the Ajax requests and provides responses. All server-side scripts used in recipes in this book have both a PHP and ColdFusion version. The recipe below, as all do, shows the PHP script installed in the URL of the Ajax call; one must only switch the file ending to `.cfm` to use the ColdFusion version. The two scripts process identically.

How to do it...

There are five main code blocks in the JavaScript; we will stop before each code block to review in detail.

```
<script type="text/javascript" src="mootools-1.3.0.js"></script>
</head>
<body>

  <div id="main">
    <h1>Mortgage ratio calculator</h1>
    <form action="javascript:" method="get" onsubmit="send_form();">
```

```
    <div id="calculator">
      <div id="screen" class="key">0</div>
      <input type="button" class="key" value="7"/>
      <input type="button" class="key" value="8"/>
      <input type="button" class="key" value="9"/>
      <input type="button" class="key" value="4"/>
      <input type="button" class="key" value="5"/>
      <input type="button" class="key" value="6"/>
      <input type="button" class="key" value="1"/>
      <input type="button" class="key" value="2"/>
      <input type="button" class="key" value="3"/>
      <input type="button" class="key" value="C"/>
      <input type="button" class="key" value="0"/>
      <input type="button" class="key" value="OK"/>
    </div>

    <div id="questions">
      <div id="question">Enter your gross, household
        monthly income:</div>
      <input type="text" id="my_number" name="gross"/>
      <input type="submit" value="Next"/>
    </div>

  </form>
</div>

<style type="text/css">
...
</style>

<script type="text/javascript">
```

▶ Setting up the listener for the key presses

We will have problems processing the data if there are unwanted characters in the data. The server-side script is ready to handle those, and makes sure that all it receives are integers, but it will help our JSON calls to not truncate comma-spliced numbers if we do some client-side processing on these values. A simple white-list procedure ensures that we only receive non-formatted, integer values. Test the key codes in your browser by adding `alert('key:'+e.key)` and seeing what is alerted when typing in the field.

```
// setup listener for the key pecks
$('my_number').addEvent('keypress',function(e) {

  white_list_keys(e); });
```

▶ Setting up the listener for the _mouse_ clicks

Whenever the mouse is clicked in the calculator made up of INPUT fields, several actions should happen based on the value clicked. If the 'OK' button is pressed, then we should transfer that value to the input field for the client. If the 'C' button is pressed, to clear the value in the calculator, then we should return the calculator screen to a zeroed-out value. Regardless of the key pressed, we make use of Element.set() to place the proper value into the inner text of the DIV that is the calculator screen.

```
// set up the listeners for the mouse pecks
  $$('.key').addEvent('click',function(e) {
    var key = this.get('value');
    var scr = $('screen').get('text');
    switch(key) {
      case 'OK':
        $('my_number').set('value',scr);
        scr = '0'; break;
      case 'C':
        scr = '0'; break;
      default:
        scr = scr+key;
        scr = scr.toInt();
    }
    $('screen').set('text',scr);
  });
```

▶ Handling the Ajax communication with the processor

Ah, the meat of the sandwich is to make some Ajax communication server-side. Since our processor is ready either to return a new question to us, or to return the final answer response, our Request.onComplete() method must be properly defined so as to handle the incoming JSON variables.

When the Ajax is fired, we will be setting some classes that hide the Next button and cause an Ajax spinner icon to appear as the background of the temporarily emptied question DIV. As a first order of onComplete business, we remove the .wait classes from those elements: $('question').removeClass('wait'); $$('input[type=submit]'). removeClass('wait');.

The next order of business is to decide how to parse the response. Using the MooTools $defined() object allows us to pass the JSON variable answer to find out if that is set. Otherwise, we will be just processing the new, incoming question.

Processing the incoming question is a simple matter of creating a new INPUT element to take input for the next question, setting the HTML of the question DIV to that of the JSON object property jsonobj.question, and then adding the event listener to white-list the key presses.

Processing the incoming answer is even easier...we no longer need anything in the `questions` DIV. So we just replace the entire thing with the incoming HTML that our Ajax, server-side processor has sent to us.

```
// handle the ajax communication with the processor
var myJax = new Request.JSON({
  url: '05_calculator.cfm',
  onComplete: function(jsonobj) {

    // clean up the waiting hoo ha
    $('question').removeClass('wait');
    $$('input[type=submit]').removeClass('wait');

    // do the question or answer work
    if (!$defined(jsonobj.answer)) {

      // inject the new question
      var new_number = new Element('input',{
        'type': 'text', 'id': 'my_number' });
      new_number.inject('question','after');
      new_number.addEvent('keypress',function(e) {
        white_list_keys(e); });
      $('question').set('html',jsonobj.question);

    } else {

      // hey! we have an answer to our calculation!
      $('questions').set('html',jsonobj.answer);

    }
  }
});
```

▶ White-listing key presses

When we bind the `keypress` function of the `my_number` DIV to our custom function, we pass the event object: `new_number.addEvent('keypress',function(e) { white_list_keys(e); });`. Our `white_list_keys()` function extends that event with the new `Event()` object in MooTools. That gives us simple, cross-browser access to `Event.key` and `Event.code`. We make use of the `e.key` property to test against our white list of `valid_chars` and then stop any unwanted input.

Server-side versus client-side validation

Server-side validation is mandatory in applications. Client-side validations, like the white-listing function earlier, are optional and *do not ever* take the place of server-side validation. Client-side validation does, however, make our application much more user friendly and responsive.

```
function white_list_keys(e) {
    var e = new Event(e);
    var valid_chars = '0123456789';
    if (
        $defined(e.key) &&        // not empty, grrr IE
        !valid_chars.contains(e.key) &&    // is white listed
        !e.key.test(/(delete|backspace|left|right)/)
    ) {
    // then do not allow this key to be typed
    e.stop();
    }
}
```

▶ Sending the form

The first item on the task list is to let our users know we have made a request server-side. The recipes in the book trade this staple of Ajax for a modicum of simplicity; nevertheless, including this is crucial if the server response is anything greater than 500 milliseconds. The `.wait` classes help us do this quickly by using `Element.addClass()`.

Some users will try to press `Next` after entering the value on the calculator. The value must be in the `INPUT` field, though. Test the `$('my_number').value.length` and grab that value, if necessary.

Transforming the existing `INPUT` variable from `type="text"` to `type="hidden"` should be child's play. Internet Explorer makes this a challenge by not allowing us to change the `type` attribute. Work around this nonsense by creating a new element using the MooTools **Element** constructor, passing it the `name`, `type`, and `value`. Inject that new element and destroy the old one: `[...].inject(el,'after'); el.destroy();`

Before we make the syntactically elegant call to our Ajax object, `myJax.send({data: data})`, we must loop through all the existing elements that should be added to `data` and use the raw JavaScript `eval()` to reconstruct the commands that build the `data` object.

```
function send_form() {

  // make the loader icon show (waiting hoo ha)
  $('question').set('text','').addClass('wait');
  $$('input[type=submit]').addClass('wait');

  // in case they press next without pressing OK
  if ($('my_number').value.length<1) {
    $('my_number').value = $('screen').get('text');
    $('screen').set('text','0');
  }

  // get the next question
  $$('input[type=text]').forEach(function(el) {

    // change the current input to hidden
    var new_hidden = new Element('input', {
      'type': 'hidden', // :( IE won't let us
        Element.set('type','hidden')
      'name': 'input_'+$$('input[type=hidden]').length,
      'value':el.value
    }).inject(el,'after');
    el.destroy(); // silly ie

    // prepare the data to be sent to the processor via ajax
    var data = {};
    $$('input[type=hidden]').forEach(function(el) {
      // use the handy "eval" to populate data
      eval('data.'+el.get('name')+'='+el.get('value'));
    });

    // make the actual ajax (json) call
    myJax.send({data:data});
  });
}

</script>
```

There's more...

We have made heavy use of a potentially unfamiliar CSS construct that grabs elements by their attribute definitions. The selector `input[type=text]` grabs all the elements that look like this in our HTML markup: `<input type="text" [...]`. Also, and now obviously, `input[type=hidden]` does the same thing for the hidden `INPUT` variables.

See also

Watch Firefox Firebug's HTML Panel where we can see the HTML markup change as we make the Ajax calls. Then also, be sure to review all the Ajax calls in the Net Panel. Note the difference in the Response and JSON areas of the POST by expanding the POST and clicking on all the subpanels.

Creating a scrolling stock ticker

Most websites that deal with financial information have some sort of scrolling mechanism that boasts information about the latest stock this-and-that. When clients come asking for one of these, we can turn to `http://www.quoterss.com/` for a free feed, or subscribe to a pay service that has even more information and may even be updated in real time.

Getting ready

First we head over to QuoteRSS.com and generate a few quote RSS feeds:

- ▶ IBM (`http://www.quoterss.com/quote.php?symbol=IBM`)

- ▶ Apple (`http://www.quoterss.com/quote.php?symbol=AAPL`)

- ▶ Google (`http://www.quoterss.com/quote.php?symbol=GOOG`)

 As we've learned previously, unless a JSON callback is implemented we cannot use externally available data. To work around the built-in, cross-domain security issues in JavaScript, we will be using a server-side script to grab our data for us.

How to do it...

We need to include the MooTools More library in this one to support the scroll:

```
<script type="text/javascript" src="mootools-1.3.0.js"></script>
  <!-- let's n0t forget the MORE -->
  <script type="text/javascript"
    src="mootools-more-1.3.0.js"></script>
</head>
<body>

  <div id="ticker_outer">
    <div id="stock_ticker">Loading...</div>
  </div>

  <style type="text/css">...</style>

  <script type="text/javascript">
...

  var myJax = new Request.JSON({

    url: '05_stock_ticker_data.php',

    onSuccess: function(jsonobj) {
      var ticker_data = '    ';
      for(key in jsonobj) {
        ticker_data += ' | '+jsonobj[key]+' | ';
      }
      $('stock_ticker').set('html',ticker_data);
      my_pics_scroller.set(0,0);
      my_pics_scroller.toRight();
    }
  });
  myJax.send();
  </script>
```

The scroll portion of this is the same as in *Chapter 4, That's Not All Folks: Animation and Scrolling*, where we scrolled pictures in a DIV. What we are adding to this is the remote request for stock data. The `Request.JSON()` class allows us to make quick work of this while creating an `onSuccess` function to run when the data returns.

It is industry-standard best practice to also code for `onFailure` and perhaps even `onCancel` given the situation.

How it works...

When the JSON data is returned and passed in as the argument to `onSuccess`, the ticker data is created piecemeal within the raw JavaScript `for (key in jasonobj)` loop.

See also

Be sure to look around the Web for what for-pay services are available that will allow a much simpler script to be written using JSON callbacks and the MooTools More **JSONP** class.

Updating a scrolling ticker periodically

Review the previous recipe; all we will be adding here is a periodic refresh that updates the data.

How to do it...

Creating a periodical object has a simple syntax that takes a mandatory first argument of how many milliseconds after which to repeat the function call.

```
// periodically (every 10 seconds) refresh the stock ticker
var refresh_ticker = function() { myJax.send(); };
var my_ticker_refresh = refresh_ticker.periodical(10*1000);

// delay (once after 30 seconds) stop the ticker refresh!
var stop_ticker_refresh = function(){
  clearInterval(my_ticker_refresh); };
stop_ticker_refresh.delay(30*1000);
```

Stopping the function call requires us to have saved the result of the periodical instantiation. In our recipe, we have saved that into the global variable `my_ticker_refresh`.

 Stopping the automatic refresh after some time may or may not be suitable for our application; however, in this example, the free feed seems to dislike us connecting to it frequently.

How it works...

This periodical object works using the raw JavaScript `setInterval()` function. The second and third arguments allow, respectively, for an object to be bound to the `this` variable within the periodic function and for arguments to be passed to the function.

There's more...

Just like `Function.periodical()`, delaying the execution of a function is made simple by using `Function.delay()`, which also takes a number of milliseconds as the mandatory parameter.

Listening to Mr. Clean's MP3 list!

Mr. Clean was a character (is a character?) in television commercials for a cleaning solution called...Ajax.

Getting ready

Mr. Clean's MP3 list resides in the same directory as this recipe, thank goodness. Before we start, we need to code a server-side script that will return the JSON list of MP3 files. Check out how to do this in `05_mp3_list.php` or `05_mp3_list.cfm` within the code snippets attached in the book. To be ready, this script must work on our server.

How to do it...

Use the `JSON()` request class to get the results from our MP3 list:

```
<script type="text/javascript" src="mootools-1.3.0.js"></script>
</head>
<body>

  <form action="javascript:" method="get">
    <input type="button" id="mybutton" value="JSON MP3 List"
      onclick="myJax.send();"/>

  </form>
  <div id="json_data"></div>

  <noscript>JavaScript is disabled.</noscript>
  <script type="text/javascript">
```

```
// request is extended with the Request.JSON class
var myJax = new Request.JSON({

    // use the google api with our domain specific api key
    url: "05_mp3_list.php",

    // receive the response from amazon
    onComplete: function(mp3_json) {
      if (!$defined(mp3_json.Error)) {

        // parse the data into html
        var stuff = '';
        for(el in mp3_json.mp3s) {
          stuff += '<br/><a href="'+mp3_json.mp3s[el]+'">
            '+mp3_json.mp3s[el]+'</a>';
        };
      } else {
        var stuff = mp3_json.Error;
      }

        // introduce the html parsed from json into the dom
        $('json_data').set('html',stuff);

    }
});
</script>
```

Then use `$defined()` to determine if the `Error` key was returned by our server-side script. Finally, the `JSON.onComplete()` method helps us loop over and parse out the MP3 links to display in the `json_data` DIV.

See also

The next recipe shows how to send a query for a particular MP3 via this same code snippet.

Querying Mr. Clean's MP3 list!

Once our MP3 list gets too long to manage, users will desire a means of sorting through the rubbish and finding only the really good tunes.

Getting ready

This recipe launches off the work we accomplished in the previous recipe. Be familiar with that and then watch for the query data to be sent to the server-side script below.

How to do it...

There is but one small change here; it only adds a few lines of code. We grab the value of the input box and pass it as the optional argument. The server-side script then cleans this value, and uses it in a matching *glob* to find files like that string:

```
function send_query() {

    // prepare the data to send
    var el = $('mp3_query');
    data = {'mp3_query':el.get('value')};

    // make the actual ajax (json) call
    myJax.send({data:data});
}
```

How it works...

In the last chapter, our *sending* widget labeled JSON MP3 List was calling myJax, the **JSON** object directly. In this example, we could create the data structure necessary to send as the optional argument from within that same onclick attribute, still, that would leave us a little claustrophobic. Instead we call a user-defined function, send_query(), which prepares the data for sending by placing it into a JSON-encoded string and then sends it along with the myJax.send({data:data}); call.

There's more...

Send the data object twice??
We are not sending the data variable twice.

We have been a bit wordy by overloading that string in this instance; however, remember that Request.send() takes a non-mandatory argument of options. One of the allowed, defined properties of that optional object is called data. We are assigning our locally defined object data to the *key* data.

[Remember our cohorts in coding when pulling a stunt like this. They will not appreciate the poetry of our coding and would much prefer to have the code read clearly!]

See also

There are numerous examples of using Ajax requests in this Web 2.0-driven world. Browse around; see how the web guys and web gals out there are making their applications more user friendly with Ajax. Then see what *we* can do to implement technology to further the business needs at our homes, churches, and offices!

6

Easy Come, Easy Go: Drag and Drop

That *dodgy* term *Web 2.0* is difficult to pin down, and this is mainly because it carries such varied meaning across its usership. Most will agree, though, that drag-and-drop usage is clearly a feature of Web 2.0.

> As we explore some ideas for using drag-and-drop that will assuredly increase the "ooh that's slick" rating of our sites, we keep in mind those that are disabled and may need to navigate using a keyboard and not a mouse. The scope of the book, however, is MooTools, so the graceful degradation will not be evident in the recipes. Attempt to always include it in your applications.

That being said, what type of cross-browser compliant drag-and-drop action will we be pursuing in this Chapter?

- ▶ Drag-and-dropping in a shopping cart implementation
- ▶ Organizing a home screen of window widgets
- ▶ Surveying of some super-sweet, sortable lists

Dragging product images around on the screen

The next few recipes will focus on an overall larger project of a drag-and-drop shopping cart interface. In this recipe, we focus on the basics of `Drag.Move()`, which handles the advanced nature of the drag-and-drop process.

How to do it...

The markup for the cart images uses a descending element hierarchy of DIV->A->IMG. We could likely do without the A tag; however, graceful degradation of the shopping cart interface would require this element. When creating the backup interface that would be used when JavaScript is not available, link this product image to a page where the item could be added to the cart without the need for client-side scripting.

For those with JavaScript, we will have quite a fancy method of adding products to the cart through the use of the Drag class object derivative Drag.Move(), using the mandatory *element* argument, which can either be a string ID from an element or a MooTools enhanced reference to an element.

```
<script  type="text/javascript"
    src="mootools-1.3.0.js"></script>
<script  type="text/javascript"
    src="mootools-more-1.3.0.js"></script>
</head>
<body>
...
  <div  id="right">
    <div  class="product"><a  id="p1">
      <img  src="06_product_1.jpg"  alt=""/></a></div>
    <div  class="product"><a  id="p2">
      <img  src="06_product_2.jpg"  alt=""/></a></div>
    <div  class="product"><a  id="p3">
      <img  src="06_product_3.jpg"  alt=""/></a></div>
    <div  class="product"><a  id="p4">
      <img  src="06_product_4.jpg"  alt=""/></a></div>
    <div  class="product"><a  id="p5">
      <img  src="06_product_5.jpg"  alt=""/></a></div>
    <div  class="product"><a  id="p6">
      <img  src="06_product_6.jpg"  alt=""/></a></div>
  </div>
  <br  clear="all"/>
  </form>

  <style  type="text/css">
...
  </style>

  <noscript>JavaScript  is  disabled.</noscript>
  <script  type="text/javascript">
  var  whereami  =  {};

  $$('div.product').each(function(el)  {
    var  aid  =  el.getFirst().get('id');
```

```
var  img_size  =  $$('#'+aid+' img')[0].getSize();
el.setStyle('height',img_size.y);
new  Drag.Move(aid,{
  droppables:  0,
  onStart:  function(el)  {
    whereami[el.get('id')]  =  el.getPosition();
  },
  onDrop:  function(el)  {
    var  put_it_back  =  function()  {
      el.setPosition(whereami[el.get('id')]);  };
      put_it_back.delay(1000);
  }
});
});
</script>
```

The following screenshot shows one of the cart items being dragged:

The second, optional argument is an object of options including:

- droppables: The element(s) on the page where the dragging element may register collisions with Drag.Move
- onStart: The function called at the very initiation of a drag-and-drop movement
- onDrop: The function called when the mouse-drag movement ends at the release of the drag

How it works...

In order to encapsulate the knowledge for this recipe, we are simply dropping the objects and then returning them to their original position. `Drag.Move.onStart()` makes use of `Element.getPosition()` to get an object of x/y values for the element on the page. We store that in the global scope variable `whereami` and use `onDrop()` to put it back.

Making use of expected behavior

Delaying the action of putting it back is Moo-riffically easy using `Function.delay()`. So we bind the function to a variable, `var put_it_back = function() { ... };`, and then call the delay object, sending it a number milliseconds to delay: `put_it_back.delay(1000)`. One thousand milliseconds, or one second, is enough time for the user to fully recognize that their drag-and-drop movement has ended, thus assuring them that the putting back of the element is expected behavior.

With any client-side trickery, most especially Ajax and drag-and-drop, that industry-beloved semantic **expected behavior** will be our guide to making a good interface. If something happens on the page that the user is not expecting, they will likely misunderstand why it is happening. We make our websites friendly by constantly measuring every action against what a user expects might or should happen under a circumstance. That measure results in the effectiveness of our application.

There's more...

The A tag in the markup is for later use, under the out-of-scope topic of graceful degradation; what is the purpose of the DIV? This recipe could certainly function with nothing but an IMG, or so it would seem. The drag-and-drop MooTool object, and all drag-and-drop modules for that matter, dynamically change the CSS style of the element to `position:absolute`. This removes the object from the DOM layout and all objects after that are moved up on the page. In our example, that would make all the images stack up upon one another and be visually very unexpected for the user.

```
var img_size = $$('#'+aid+' img')[0].getSize();
el.setStyle('height',img_size.y);
```

On instantiation of `Drag.Move()`, the image size is recorded from the MooTool object `Element.getSize()`, which returns x/y values for the element. Unlike `Element.getPosition()` which gives x/y values based on the position on the page, these x/y values are the height and width of the object. Using those values to set the height of the relatively positioned DIV allows our page layout to remain unchanged.

See also

A frequent error on the part of all of us is to go directly to the documentation. Well, let us clarify that. Reviewing the documentation for `Drag.Move()` is *expected behavior*. Nevertheless, not reviewing the base class for `Drag.Move()` would leave us with a half-understanding of what the extended object is truly capable of. Review `Drag()` in the MooTools documentation `http://mootools.net/docs/more/Drag/Drag`.

Making a shopping cart where products can be dropped

If we are joining this recipe from the previous example in this chapter, we are ready. The overall shopping cart recipe starts in the first recipe in *Chapter 6, Easy Come, Easy Go: Drag and Drop*.

How to do it...

To progress from a page where product images can be moved around to a shopping cart interface where product images can be dropped in a holding area, we first add the listeners that notify us that we are or are not dragging to a location that is defined as the shopping cart `cart`. These functions of `Drag.Move()` are named `onEnter()` and `onLeave()`.

```
    <script type="text/javascript"
      src="mootools-1.3.0.js"></script>
    <script type="text/javascript"
      src="mootools-more-1.3.0.js"></script>
</head>
<body>

    <form id="myform" action="javascript:" method="post">
    <h1>My Big Store o' Stuff</h1>
    <h2>Cutting prices and all that booyah!</h2>
    <small>You are here:</small> <strong>shopping ->
      stuff -> more stuff</strong><br/>

    <div id="left">
      <small>My Cart:</small>
      <div id="hitter"></div>
    </div>
...
    <script type="text/javascript">
    var whereami = {};
    $$('div.product').each(function(el) {
      var aid = el.getFirst().get('id');
      var img_size = $$('#'+aid+' img')[0].getSize();
      el.setStyle('height',img_size.y);
      new Drag.Move(aid,{
        droppables: '#hitter',
        onStart: function(el) {
          whereami[el.get('id')] = el.getPosition();
      },
        onDrop: function(el) {
          if (!el.hasClass('in-cart')) {
            var put_it_back = function() {
              el.setPosition(whereami[el.get('id')]); };
            put_it_back.delay(1000);
          } else {
      //  the drop zone may have a static
            height (when empty)
            $('hitter').setStyle('height','auto');

      // firstly, put back the element we're dragging
            var dragid = el.get('id');
            el.setPosition(whereami[dragid]);
```

```
        // we need a copy of the picture to put in the cart
            var clone_product = el.clone();
            clone_product.setStyles(
               {'left':0,'top':0,'position':'relative'});

        // id's need to be unique and the pic should be smaller
            var newid = String.uniqueID()+'__'+dragid;
            clone_product.set('id',newid).
               getFirst().setStyle('width','85px');

        // put the new item in the cart
            $('hitter').grab(clone_product);
         }
      },
      onEnter: function(el) {
        el.addClass('in-cart');
        $('left').addClass('in');
      },
      onLeave: function(el) {
        el.removeClass('in-cart');
        $('left').addClass('in');
      }
    });
  });
</script>
```

Within these two methods, onEnter and onLeave, we turn on or off a class that will mark this element as either being in or *not being in* the droppable area.

How it works...

Altering the action in Drag.Move.onDrop() based on whether or not the class exists allows us to either put the item back into the items DIV, at the right, or to clone it and place it relatively positioned within the droppable hitter area.

There's more...

We continue this shopping cart experience in the drag-and-drop dimension in the next recipe where we change the onscreen inventory levels as the products are added.

Changing onscreen inventory levels when a product is dropped on the cart

The first two recipes in this chapter lead up to the complexity found in this example. Those familiar with the concepts will find the client-side inventory level tracking quite easy to follow.

How to do it

In order to display the inventory and quantity levels, the HTML markup changed slightly. We note that important change as we proceed with the tracking of quantities.

```
<script  type="text/javascript"
   src="mootools-1.3.0.js"></script>
<script  type="text/javascript"
   src="mootools-more-1.3.0.js"></script>
</head>
<body>
...
  <div  id="left">
    <small>My  Cart:</small>
    <div  id="hitter"><br  clear="both"/></div>
  </div>
  <div  id="right">
    <div  class="product"><a  id="p1">
    <img  src="06_product_1.jpg"  alt=""/>
    <br/>Inventory:
      <span  class="inventory">5689</span></a></div>
...
  </div>
  <br  clear="all"/>
  </form>

  <style  type="text/css">
...
  #left.in  {  border:3px  solid  #ABABAB;  }
  #hitter  a.in-cart  {  width:85px;
    display:block;  float:left;  }
  #hitter  a.in-cart  img  {  width:85px;  }
  </style>

  <script  type="text/javascript">
  var  whereami  =  {};
```

```
$$('div.product').each(function(el) {
  var aid = el.getFirst().get('id');
  var img_size = $$('#'+aid+' img')[0].getSize();
  el.setStyle('height',img_size.y);
  new Drag.Move(aid,{
    droppables: '#hitter',
    onStart: function(el) { ... },
    onDrop: function(el) {
      if (!el.hasClass('in-cart')) {
        var put_it_back = function() {
          el.setPosition(whereami[el.get('id')]); };
        put_it_back.delay(1000);
      } else {

  // remove hitting indicator
...
  // firstly, put back the element we're dragging
...
  // we need a copy of the picture to put in the cart
...
  // id's need to be unique and the pic should be smaller
...

  // remove any duplicates
        var src = clone_product.getFirst().get('src');
        $$('#hitter img[src='+src+']').
        getParent().destroy();

  // put the new item in the cart
        $('hitter').grab(clone_product,'top');

  // change the Inventory level to a count of that product
        var cloned_html = $(newid).get('html');
        cloned_html = cloned_html.replace(
          /Inventory/m,'Quantity');
        $(newid).set('html',cloned_html);


  // client side storage!
        if ($$('.'+dragid).length==1) {
          var qty = $$('.'+dragid)[0].
          get('value').toInt()
          $$('.'+dragid)[0].set('value',++qty);
        } else {
```

```
        var  qty  =  1;
        new  Element('input',  {
          'type':'hidden',
          'name':dragid,
          'class':dragid,
          'value':qty
        }).inject('hitter','bottom');
      }
      $$('#'+newid+'  .inventory').set('text',qty);

// change the quantity in the cart and the inventory on the page
        var  inventory  =  $$('#'+dragid+'  .
          inventory')[0].get('text');
        var  new_inventory_level  =  inventory-1;
        $$('#'+dragid+'  .inventory').
          set('text',new_inventory_level);
        if  (new_inventory_level<1)  el.removeEvents();


      }
    },
    onEnter:  function(el)  {  ...  },
    onLeave:  function(el)  {  ...  }
  }
});
});
</script>
```

How it works...

▸ Remove any duplicates and put the item in the cart.

To this point in the recipe, we are simply using the previous recipe's information. Check back in the previous recipe for information on how to handle the cart to this point in the current recipe.

▸ Change the Inventory level to a count of that product.

Grabbing the HTML of newid allows us to change the DIV metadata about the product from that of an Inventory level to that of a Quantity level. The regular expression /Inventory/m is used to replace that string with the string Quantity. The "m" indicates that the pattern should be found across multiple lines of text.

▶ Store the inventory in the DOM for easy reference.

Storing the inventory in memory would be one way to handle this; however, experience with developing tricky interfaces teaches that having a visible reference of what is going on is invaluable and lowers maintenance costs drastically. Grab the value of the quantity stored from a hidden input variable, or create it if it does not yet exist. Also, set the text of the inventory DIV to the appropriate quantity.

▶ Change the quantity in the cart and the inventory on the page.

Most of our work is done: the image is cloned in place with duplicates removed and the quantity level is updated in the cart and stored in the DOM. Now we need to grab the proper element that our user had been dragging and update the inventory level to show the quantity (one) removed from the virtual shelf. Fortunately, we still have access to the ID of the element we were dragging. Update the quantity garnered from the inner text of the inventory span and then update the same element with the new quantity. Be sure to remove the events from any element whose quantity has fallen to zero.

There's more...

Some may find that a cart that shows one of each item in the cart is good eye-candy. It clearly shows how many we have and mimics real life, in that, if we put three sleeping bags in our cart at the local market, there will not be a magic number 3 hovering over a single sleeping bag box. Still, to track the levels, let us use the magic quantity tracker and show only one of each product. To do that we need to remove duplicate images while simultaneously tracking the quantity level.

The removal of any item is elementary using `Element.destroy()` and in conjunction with the double dollar object, we can quickly create a dynamic CSS string that grabs all images that have the same source as the image that our user is dragging into the cart `$$('#hitter img[src='+src+']').getParent().destroy()`.

We need a pocket to safely store our quantity level. While Ajax is a great solution for this, and we accomplish that in the next recipe, let us move forward slowly by using the simplest client-side storage possible: *hidden INPUT elements*!

The product inventory ID is cleverly concealed within the ID of the A tag surrounding our product image. We can make use of that again; however, since IDs must be unique, we use that as a class attribute. Finding the quantity in our cart for product "p1" is now as easy as grabbing the current value of `$$('.p1')[0].get('value')`.

Allowing products in a shopping cart to be "put back" on the shelf

Having a firm grasp on the previous three recipes that are building blocks for what is happening in this example keeps us on track.

How to do it...

There is very little to removing the cart items. Our most difficult part is adding a widget with which our users will remove the products. The PNG format image with transparency is supported in all major browsers and adds a flair of professionalism to the cart.

```
...
// change the Inventory level to a count of that product
var cloned_html = $(newid).get('html');
cloned_html = cloned_html.replace(
  /Inventory/m,'Quantity');
$(newid).set('html',cloned_html);

// add a return to shelf X at top right of each contaier
new Element('a',{
  class: 'back_to_shelf'
}).addEvent('click',function() {
// remove the hidden, client-side storage, INPUT vars
  $$('.'+dragid).destroy();
// remove the picture from the cart
  this.getParent().destroy();
}).inject(newid,'top');

// client side storage!
if ($$('.'+dragid).length==1) {
...
```

How it works...

Recalling that both changing the inventory level and "client-side storage!" are segments of the recipe explained previously in this chapters, we focus on **adding a return-to-shelf image**, an "x", at the upper-right corner of the image. The style, class: 'back_to_shelf', which is used to display the return to shelf widget, floats the image above the layout position: absolute and then moves it to the right margin-left:60px.

Two methods are chained to the new element construct: `Element.addEvent()` and `Element.inject()`. Before injecting the new element into the DOM, we are able to use the MooTools function binding `addEvent()` to destroy the hidden, client-side storage, which is the related hidden INPUT variable found within the DIV `#hitter`. After that, we traverse the DOM up a single level from the "x" widget to its parent whose inner HTML has all the information presenting the item in the cart. Its removal concludes the "back to shelf" process.

See also

The snippet here is very short; be sure to review the previous recipes for the bigger picture of how the shopping cart is being created from scratch using MooTools, HTML, and CSS. The code snippets included with the book are complete.

Making Ajax calls when products are dropped or added to a shopping cart

We are in the fifth stand-alone example of a project we have built in sections from the beginning of the chapter. Being familiar with the concepts and ideas of those other recipes readies us for the minor addition of Ajax.

How to do it...

Before we can call the Ajax, the request must be instantiated with some options. The most important option is the URL to the server-side script. Choosing a method of either POST or GET could be a personal preference or may be a decision already made by corporate guidelines or culture. Being sure that a client that has lost connectivity is not confused over downstream unexpected behavior is solved using `Request.onFailure()`, which can handle the optional argument of the XHR response.

```
var shoppingJax = new Request({
  url: '06_shopping_ajax.php',
  method: 'post',
  onFailure: function() {
    alert('There may have been an error.
      Please check your Internet connection.');
  },
});
...
  // put the new item in the cart
  $('hitter').grab(clone_product,'top');

  // send ajax to a server-side script
  // what product are we sending?
  var data = {
    'product':dragid,'action':'add'};
```

```
    shoppingJax.send({data:data});
...
    // remove the hidden, client-side storage, INPUT vars
    $$('.'+dragid).destroy();

    // send ajax to a server-side script
    // what product are we sending?
    var data = {
        'product':dragid,'action':'remove'};
    shoppingJax.send({data:data});
```

How it works...

In the `Request.send()` call, we send the data to act upon as an encoded object. The object encoding is key-value pairs created from the `dragid`, which in our cart design is the product inventory number preceded by the letter "p" and the action we are taking, whether it be to "add" the product within the server-side script, meaning to remove one more product from inventory, or the reverse, "remove", signaling for the inventory to regain that product in the shelf inventory.

There's more...

MooTools Ajax is implemented through an object class called `Request()`. From `Request()` are spawned extensions like `Request.HTML()` and `Request.JSON()`. Our template server-side script does nothing more than echo out the values of what it is sent. Code that server-side script to contact the database for the shopping cart and update the stored inventory levels.

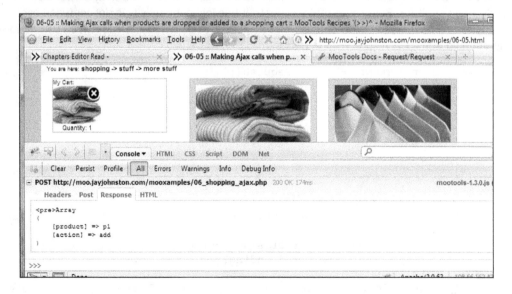

The image shows the FireFox Firebug Net Panel where the Ajax call has gone to the server-side script and the response has been returned.

Making a reset button to remove all products from a shopping cart

This is the last recipe in this series. Please join us from the first recipe through the fifth by beginning at the first page of *Chapter 6, Easy Come, Easy Go: Drag and Drop.*

How to do it...

Adding just a couple of lines in a few key places set us up to remove all the cart business logic and presentation logic that is being stored client-side for our user.

▶ Adding a widget to remove all items

```
<a  id="clear_all_trigger">Remove  All  Products</a>
<style  type="text/css">
    #clear_all_trigger  {  cursor:pointer;  font-color:#00F;
      text-decoration:underline;  }
<style>
```

When placing the widget, we give some thought to design and align the text left, color it, and so on. What is **more important**, though, is that our widget needs to appear clickable. Any HTML A tag without the HREF attribute will not appear as clickable. Setting the style `cursor:pointer;` solves that usability issue.

▶ Making the widget remove the items

There are two sets of items we need to remove. The hidden input variables in `#hitter` that are storing our product counts must have their values sent server-side via Ajax so that the inventory levels will be updated by the server-side script. The other set of items are the presentation side of that client-side storage. Removing all the A tags with `display` set to `block` removes the mini-pictures of cart items as well as the associated quantity text.

```
$('clear_all_trigger').addEvent('click',function()  {
    //  for  each  product  in  our  "client  side  storage"
    $$('#hitter  input[type=hidden]').each(function(el,i)  {
        //  get  each  product  id
        var  product_id  =  el.get('class');
        //  get  the  count  for  each  as  well
        var  product_qty  =  el.get('value');
        //  ajax  the  requests  back
        var  data  =  {'product':product_id,'action':
          'remove','quantity':product_qty};
```

```
            shoppingJax.send({data:data});
            // remove the element from the cart
            el.destroy();
        });
        $$('a.in-cart').destroy();
        $('hitter').setStyle('height','200px');
    });
```

▸ Whoops! Saving our main product photos

Those of us following line-by-line in the code snippet have already seen the fix. Those of us that have only added the two previous blocks of code have found that the main product images disappear when the `$$('a.in-cart').destroy()` is called.

Early on, the block that switches on the class `in-cart`, from within the `onDrop()` function, paid no attention to the fact the `in-cart` class was left on the main image. Add a line of code at the bottom of that `onDrop`, `else` code block to remove the `in-cart` class.

```
// forgetting to remove this will cause the remove all button to
    be greedy!
el.removeClass('in-cart');
```

See also

To complete this shopping cart, the server-side script will have to have database interaction with a MySQL, MSSQL, or other database datastore to both initially retrieve and on-the-fly update the cart inventory, not to mention process sales from the cart. Packt Publishing, has a great book on PHP E-commerce, `https://www.packtpub.com/php-5-e-commerce-development/book`.

Dragging window widgets around on a screen

Let us face it, visitors go ga-ga over dragging and transparency. So let us add some transparency to our window widget module and drag it around the screen for effect.

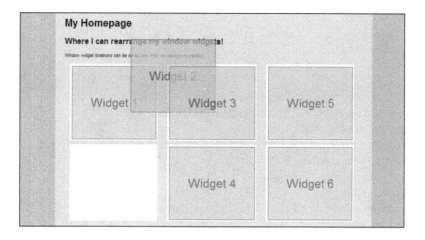

Getting ready

Get ready to create some intelligent window widgets! Remember to include both MooTools Core and the MooTools More in the head of our document.

How to do it...

Use a collection of elements to place drag-and-drop code on a group of like items.

```
<div id="page">
  <h1>My Homepage</h1>
  <h2>Where I can rearrange my window widgets!</h2>
  <small><em>Window widget locations can be saved
    only after an account is created.</em></small><br/>
  <div id="left">
    <div class="hitter"><div class="widget" id="w1">
      Widget 1</div></div>
    <div class="hitter"><div class="widget" id="w2">
      Widget 2</div></div>
  </div>
  <div id="center">
    <div class="hitter"><div class="widget" id="w3">
      Widget 3</div></div>
    <div class="hitter"><div class="widget" id="w4">
      Widget 4</div></div>
  </div>
  <div id="right">
    <div class="hitter"><div class="widget" id="w5">
      Widget 5</div></div>
    <div class="hitter"><div class="widget" id="w6">
```

```
      Widget  6</div></div>
  </div>
<br  clear="all"/>
</div>

<style  type="text/css">
body  {  background-color:#ABABAB;  font-size:11px;
  font-family:arial;  }
#page  {  margin:0  auto;  width:640px;  padding:20px;
  background-color:#CDCDCD;  }
#left,  #center,  #right  {  float:left;  width:200px;
  margin:5px;  }
.hitter  {  width:190px;  height:160px;  margin:5px;
  border:1px  solid  #BCBCBC;  background-color:#FFF;  }
.widget  {  width:180px;  height:150px;  margin:5px;
  border:1px  solid  #00F;  background-color:#ABABAB;
  font-size:25px;  line-height:150px;  text-align:center;  }
</style>

<script  type="text/javascript">
var  whereami  =  {};
$$('.widget').each(function(el)  {
  whereami[el.get('id')]  =  el.getCoordinates();
  var  widget_id  =  el.get('id');
  new  Drag.Move(widget_id,{
    droppables:  0,
    onStart:  function(el)  {
      el.setStyle('opacity',.7);
    },
    onDrop:  function(el)  {
      el.setStyle('opacity',1);
      var  put_it_back  =  function()  {
        el.setPosition(whereami[el.get('id')]);  };
      put_it_back.delay(1000);
    }
  });
</script>
```

How it works...

The HTML layout requires at least two items. There must be a group of widgets that we will be pushing around the screen. They, in turn, must have a parent element that is positioned relatively, so that the DOM does not fold up and all widgets end up on top of one another.

Instantiate the draggable elements by looping over the widget collection.

Collections and Elements

As a rule of thumb, if we need to do something to a group of elements, we assign classes to them and grab them with a CSS string sent through the collection object, `$$()` like this: `$$('.widget')`. That dot (.) at the beginning of the string is a class indicator. If we are grabbing a single element, we use the single dollar object, `$()`.

The `$$().each` method loops over each element in a collection. The element is passed in as the first argument to the bound function, "el" here: `$$('.widget').each(function(el) { ... }`. That gives us direct access to the element like `el[i]` within a raw JavaScript `for(i in el)` . . . .

There's more...

In the next recipe, we further extend what we have accomplished in this recipe by adding actions to the `onDrop` and `onStart` methods.

Making window widgets push other widgets around on a screen

Launching off our foundation from the previous recipe, we now get ready to have window widgets magically switch places. This will act like a game of musical chairs where when one widget moves into the place of a second, the second takes the place of the first. And unlike musical chairs, no widget loses and has to sit down until the next round.

How to do it...

The structure of the `Drag.Move()` object is the same. Added in this recipe is the functionality of the `onEnter` and `onLeave` events. Note how the hitters now have a class added upon entering and that class removed upon leaving to create a highlight effect. This tells the user they have dragged an item to a hittable zone.

```
$$('.widget').each(function(el) {
  whereami[el.get('id')] = el.getCoordinates();
  var widget_id = el.get('id');
  new Drag.Move(widget_id,{
    droppables: $$('.hitter'),
    onStart: function(el) {
      el.setStyle('opacity',.7);
    },
```

```
     onDrop:  function(el,hitter)  {
       el.setStyle('opacity',1);
       var  put_it_back  =  function()  {
         el.setStyles(whereami[el.get('id')]);   };
       put_it_back.delay(1000);
       hitter.removeClass('over');
     },
     onEnter:  function(el,hitter)  {
       if  (hitter)  {
         hitter.addClass('over');
         var  incumbent  =  hitter.getFirst();
         if  (incumbent)  {
           // take  role  call
           var  dragid  =  el.get('id');
           var  incumbentid  =  incumbent.get('id');

           // document  where  they  were  at  load
           var  dragdestination  =
             whereami[incumbentid];
           var  incumbentdestination  =
             whereami[dragid];

           // switch  their  places
           whereami[incumbentid]  =
             incumbentdestination;
           whereami[dragid]  =  dragdestination;

           // make  them  switch
           incumbent.setStyles(incumbentdestination);
           var  adopter  =  incumbent.getParent();
           el.getParent().grab(incumbent);
           adopter.grab(el);
         }
       }
     },
     onLeave:  function(el,hitter)  {
       hitter.removeClass('over');
     }
   });
});
```

How it works...

The trick to this *switcheroo* is four part. Firstly, using the second argument to the `onEnter` method, we have access to the element that is the zone being hit. In other words, the hitter is the element that has been registered as a droppable zone and it is turning bright yellow to let the user know that, too!

Next we grab the original coordinates of each of the two items that we need to switch. They were stored in `whereami` during the initial page load with the ID attribute of the element as the array index.

After switching the locations in our `whereami` documentation of the coordinates on page, we then have their respective parents fill out the adoption papers à la `Element.grab()`, which causes the actual elements in the DOM to change places. See in this image where the parent hitters for "w1" and "w3" are switching places as w1 is dragged over to the w3 hitter.

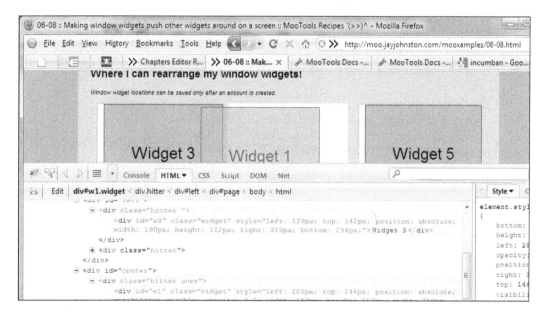

See also

This switcheroo is fast; it happens like lightning. Watch in Firefox Firebug as a widget is dragged from one hitter zone to the next! The next recipe shows how to add Ajax calls that could be used to record a user's widget location preferences.

Making Ajax calls to record the location of window widgets

Following along with the work we have done in the past three recipes on the draggable window widgets, we ready ourselves to send the window locations via Ajax to a server-side script that could be easily made to store a user's window and widget locations in a database.

How to do it...

Thus far, we did not need to know the locations of the hitters. The widget movement has been independent of the hitter it was landing in. Now, to record that data, name the hitters with unique ID attributes.

```
<div  id="left">
   <div  class="hitter"  id="loc1">
   <div  class="widget"  id="w1">Widget  1</div></div>
   <div  class="hitter"  id="loc2">
   <div  class="widget"  id="w2">Widget  2</div></div>
</div>
<div  id="center">
   <div  class="hitter"  id="loc3">
   <div  class="widget"  id="w3">Widget  3</div></div>
   <div  class="hitter"  id="loc4">
   <div  class="widget"  id="w4">Widget  4</div></div>
</div>
<div  id="right">
   <div  class="hitter"  id="loc5">
   <div  class="widget"  id="w5">Widget  5</div></div>
   <div  class="hitter"  id="loc6">
   <div  class="widget"  id="w6">Widget  6</div></div>
</div>
```

With the hitters having unique names and the widgets having unique names, we can simply take the inventory of the data and then send it to our script. In the code snippet included with the book, the server-side script simply echoes what is sent to it.

```
onDrop:  function(el,hitter)  {
  el.setStyle('opacity',1);
  var  put_it_back  =  function()  {
    el.setStyles(whereami[el.get('id')]);  };
  put_it_back.delay(1000);
  hitter.removeClass('over');
```

```
    // create an object of widget locations
    var data = {};
    $$('.hitter').each(function(el) {
      var hitter_loc = el.get('id');
      var incumbent = el.getFirst().get('id');
      eval('data.'+hitter_loc+' = incumbent');
    });
    // record it
    widgetJax.send({data:data});
  },
```

How it works...

The `onDrop` method has one small block added to it that loops over the collection of elements that have the class hitter, `$$('.hitter').each(function(el) { ... }`. Grabbing the hitter and incumbent widget IDs are child's play with MooTools' `Element.get()`, and we once again make use of `eval()` trickery to make dynamic variables for the six hitters. The result in Firefox's Firebug Net Panel looks like this after moving widget 1 into widget 3's position:

<pre>Array

(

  [loc1] => w3

  [loc2] => w2

  [loc3] => w1

  [loc4] => w4

  [loc5] => w5

  [loc6] => w6

)

See also

In the final recipe in this draggable window-widget adventure, we recognize the age-old saying, "Easy come, easy go", by creating a single-click button that will return all window widgets to their original positions. Easy drag, easy reset?

Making a reset button to put widgets back into a default state

Those that have been rocking the window widgets along for the past three recipes are embodied with unmistakable readiness!

How to do it...

In the Ajax recipe for the window widgets, we placed a block of code within `onDrop` that was meant to create an object containing the widget locations and send that data server-side for processing. When our reset widget, `<input type="button" value="Reset All" id="reset"/>` is pressed, we will need to call that same block of code. Start by moving it into its own function.

```
function record_locations() {
  // create an object of widget locations
  var data = {};
  $$('.hitter').each(function(el) {
    var hitter_loc = el.get('id');
    var incumbent = el.getFirst().get('id');
    eval('data.'+hitter_loc+' = incumbent');
  });
  // record it
  widgetJax.send({data:data});
}
```

 That is the same block of code, and it is now reusable as a custom function.

The next order of business to reset the window locations is to keep a record of where they are at load. Making of a copy of an object in JavaScript is made easy by MooTools' `Object.clone()` method.

```
// prepare to reset to original location
var whereWASi = Object.clone(whereami);
```

With the `whereWASi` variable in place, we add the `click` event to our bound function.

```
// reset on click to original location
$('reset').addEvent('click',function() {
  $$('.widget').each(function(el) {
    // identify widget
    var wid = el.get('id');
```

```
    // identify parent hitter (locid_#)
    var pid = wid.replace(/w/,'loc');
    // reset visible location
    el.setStyles(whereWASi[wid]);
    // effect adoption by 1st parent
    $(pid).grab(el);
  });
  // record it server-side
  record_locations();
});
```

How it works...

The collection containing the widgets, $$('.widget'), is made from a CSS selector that grabs all elements with the class *widget*. Looping over those elements, we identify the widget by using Element.get() to get the ID attribute value. The parent hitter is also required in order for us to reset the locations and is identified by replacing the *w* with *loc*, thus taking advantage of our simple naming convention.

The variable whereWASi has as its value a complete record of all the original locations. Those values are needed to reset the styles of each widget to the original page-load state. Having the original parent adopt the element allows the record_locations() function to send the new, original widget locations server-side for processing.

There's more...

The two terms "passing by reference" and "passing by value" have important consideration when we are trying to make a copy of a variable. One may ask why the cloning of the whereami object had to be done via something other than straight assignment, like var whereWASi = whereami. The answer is that simple variables in JavaScript are passed by value whereas objects are passed by reference.

See also

Jonathan Snook explains this very well in his article at snook.ca: http://snook.ca/archives/javascript/javascript_pass.

Creating a sortable list

MooTools has sweet utilities that most have never even realized they needed. Hang on for a recipe that makes you want to shout, "Hey, I didn't know you could do that!".

Getting ready

Be sure to include both the MooTools Core and the MooTools More for this recipe.

How to do it...

Create a list to sort.

```
<ol  id="mylist"  style="line-height:25px;cursor:pointer;">
  <li>Oldies-but-Goodies:  Foundational  Moo</li>
  <li>Switching  Paddles  Midstream:  Changing  HTML
    After  Page  Load</li>
...
  <li>I'll  Gladly  Pay  Tue.  For  Moo  Today:  Extensions
    on  the  Web</li>
  <li>Electric  Milk:  Plugins  and  More</li>
</ol>
```

Then ask MooTools to make it sortable.

```
<script  type="text/javascript">
  var  list  =  new  Sortables('mylist');
</script>
```

Grab, drag, sort, and shout, "Wheeeee!".

How it works...

This is a nifty extension of `Drag.move()`, which serializes DOM elements during the drag process.

There's more...

This extension can do so much. In the next recipe, we show how to implement some of the methods available as the second parameter to the constructor.

Sending sorted list info via Ajax

The last recipe prepared us, with just a single line of MooScript, to a point that we are now ready to send sorted list info via Ajax. Create a server-side script that will connect to a database and store a user's list information. We will use that script info in the `url` property of the Ajax call.

How to do it...

The `Sortables()` class takes options in the secondary, optional argument. Adding in an `onComplete()` function allows for actions to be taken once a sort has occurred.

```
<script  type="text/javascript">
    var  list  =  new  Sortables('mylist',{
      onComplete:  function()  {
      //  create  an  object  of  widget  locations
      var  data  =  {};
      $$('#mylist  li').each(function(el,index)  {
        var  list_item  =  el.get('id');
        eval('data.pos_'+index+'  =  "'+list_item+'"');
      });
      sortJax.send({data:data});
      }
    });
    var  sortJax  =  new  Request({
      url:  '06_shopping_ajax.php',
      method:  'post',
      onFailure:  function()  {
        alert('There  may  have  been  an  error.
          Please  check  your  Internet  connection.');
      },
    });
</script>
```

The Ajax request is prepared in the global scope using the MooTools object `Request()`. Assign the proper server-side script to `Request.url`. The Ajax object, `sortJax` is sent from within the `onComplete` function once the list items have been converted into a data object. The data object is passed via `Request.send()` here: `sortJax.send({data:data})`.

7
Knock and the Door Will Open: Events and Listeners

In exploration of the Web 2.0 frontier, it is quite notable that pages no longer sit, statically starting back at users, waiting silently for the next hyperlink click that will send a clunky HTTP refresh and cause the page to change.

Events are actions, for instance a user clicking on a page element. To *Listen* for this action we create a listener, which is an action bound to an event. The actions are functions or object methods that are bound to HTML events. These events have keyword definitions, to name a few `onClick`, `onFocus`, and `onChange`.

And now, the main event...events, which include:

- ▶ Standard and custom HTML events fired by the DOM
- ▶ Bound listeners that encapsulate kinetic energies waiting to be unleashed
- ▶ Event chains that are handy, user friendly, and even polite!

Creating an event listener that "hello"s on click

Getting ready

To say "Hello World" using a technique that causes elements to stand at our beck and call, we must be sure our HTML DOM is complete and syntactically valid, and then we add an element that will be our trigger:

```
<input type="button" id="mybutton" value="Greet Me!"/>
```

How to do it...

Place a listener on that trigger element using `Element.addEvent()` and pass it an anonymous function to bind to the event:

```
var  mygreeting = 'Hello  World!';
var  onEvent = 'click';  // do not include the "on" in onClick
  $('mybutton').addEvent(onEvent,function(myevent)  {
     // extend the event with MooTools, we may stop the event
     var  e  =  new  Event(myevent);
     e.stop();
     // let  us  say  hello  in  a  few  different  ways
     $('mycanvas').set('text',mygreeting); // 1 write to DOM
     alert(mygreeting);                     // 2 pop up  modal
     window.status  =  mygreeting;          // 3  window status
     console.log(mygreeting);               // 4 write to console
  });
```

Three of the four actions called are visible in this image:

How it works...

When the trigger is clicked, the HTML DOM *checks in* with all listeners for that event. Since MooTools helped us `addEvent()` `onClick` to the `mytrigger` INPUT element, that event, `onClick`, fires the anonymous function that contains the four actions.

There's more...

The function passed to `addEvent()`, itself has been passed a single argument. Though this actual event itself is not needed in our example, frequently, we need to stop that event or act upon it in some other way. Extend it with MooTools **Event** construct.

See also

Read about all the goodies the MooTools event is infused with:
`http://mootools.net/docs/core/Types/Event`.

Removing a listener that responds to clicks

To release an element from our beck and call when it is no longer needed, we need to have first added an event to it. Since we start this recipe with the *Hello World* from the previous one, we are ready to remove the event.

Getting ready

We still keep in mind that `mybutton` will be triggering the action in this recipe.

```
<input  type="button"  id="mybutton"  value="Greet  Me!"/>
```

How to do it...

First, add a widget called `mycancel` and provide an `onclick` attribute that handles the click event. This bound function uses the MooTools `Element.removeEvents()` without the optional argument of which types of events to remove and therefore removes them all.

```
<input type="button" id="mycancel" value="Okay, nevermind"
  onclick="
    $('mybutton').removeEvents();
    alert('We  will  no  longer  say  Hello');
"/>
```

How it works...

On page load, the element with ID `mybutton` had an event added to it; upon every click, it *said "hello"* in four different ways. Removing that event means that when our button is now clicked, it will do nothing.

There's more...

To make the recipe more effective, it seems necessary to have the HELLOs removed shortly after issuing them. Use MooTools `Funtion.delay()` with the mandatory argument of milliseconds to delay for this purpose.

```
// after a delay of 1 second, remove our hellos
  var cleanup = (function clear_hello() {
        $('mycanvas').set('text','');
        window.status = '';
  }).delay(1000);
```

Creating a group of elements that add their NAMEs and VALUEs as text in a DIV

Often in dynamic DOM manipulation of a web form, we must check the contents of the DOM using a live HTML debugger like Firefox's Firebug HTML Panel. This recipe is for those ready to have a quick look at a particular group of hidden elements. Get ready to turn on the light and watch the critters scatter; they're not so hidden anymore!

Getting ready

Start with a form that has hidden elements that we can mine for display.

```
<form id="myform" action="">
        <input type="button" value="Show values"/>
        <input type="hidden" name="h_1" value="Matthew"/>
        <input type="hidden" name="h_2" value="Mark"/>
 . . .
```

How to do it...

Grab the `INPUT` button that is within the form and attach a listener to it. Define that listener to loop over a collection of `#myform input[type=hidden]` elements, the `INPUT` elements within the form `myform` that are explicitly marked with `type="hidden"`.

```
$$('#myform input[type=button]').addEvent('click',
   function()  {
      $('mycanvas').set('html','');
      $$('#myform  input[type=hidden]').each(function(el)  {
         var  canvastext  =  $('mycanvas').get('html');
         var text2addon = el.get('name')+'='+el.get('value');
         var text2addon .= '<br/>';
         $('mycanvas').set('html',canvastext+text2addon);
      });
   ...
});
```

How it works...

Each time the `onClick` listener bound to `#myform input[type=button]` fires, the DIV with ID `mycanvas` is emptied and then repopulated during that loop. That loop grabs the `NAME` and `VALUE` attributes of the hidden `INPUT` elements and appends them to the inner HTML of `mycanvas`.

There's more...

The last recipe showed a way to bind a function to a variable and execute the MooTools `Function.delay()` method on it. Look at this more compact version that is syntactically more foreign but accomplishes the same delay in fewer characters.

```
// an abbreviated version of the last recipe's clear function
(function(){  $('mycanvas').set('html','');  }).delay(1000);
```

Responding to both CLICK and MOUSEOVER

Getting ready

Remember `mybutton`? We will be using that as our trigger again.

```
<input  type="button"  id="mybutton"  value="Greet  Me!"/>
```

How to do it...

Using the same triggering `INPUT` widget and hello-saying lines of code from earlier in this chapter, we are ready to add multiple events to `mybutton`.

```
$('mybutton').addEvents({
    'click':say_hello,
    'mouseover':say_hello
});
```

How it works...

After moving the lines of code that must be reused, the lines that greet our user in four different ways, we have functionally encapsulated these actions. We then use MooTools' `Element.addEvents()` to add multiple event listeners that will call the `say_hello()` function.

Removing one of multiple event listeners

Getting ready

Keep in mind that `mybutton` is the trigger for our actions in this recipe.

```
<input type="button" id="mybutton" value="Greet Me!"/>
```

How to do it...

Continuing from the previous recipe where we have associated both click and mouseover actions to a triggering `INPUT` button, we prepare to remove some, but not all, events.

```
$('mybutton').removeEvents('mouseover');
```

How it works...

The object function `Element.removeEvents()` when used without any optional arguments will remove all events bound to an element. Passing in the single argument "mouseover" causes all events bound to that event action to be removed. This allows for the `onClick()` action previously bound to continue to function while preventing the `onMouseover()` action entirely.

There's more...

MooTools has two methods in the `Element` class that are used for removing events. `Element.removeEvent()` takes two mandatory arguments. Like `removeEvents()`, the first parameter indicates which action is being specified in the call. The second parameter is the function to unbind.

See also

All avid MooTool users are familiar with `http://mootools.net/docs/core/Element/Element.Event`, as the methods described are key to making web pages interactive.

Adding another event listener to an element

Often in object oriented code practice, defined events are found within separate encapsulations but may require being bound to the same element. In this recipe we look at how to make multiple `addEvent()` calls, not only to the same element, but upon the same bound event action.

Getting ready

This recipe uses code from the previous Chapter 7 "Hello World" recipes. A review of those recipes will have us ready to add events to the same element, same event action.

And, of course, we call upon `mybutton` to trigger our actions.

```
<input type="button" id="mybutton" value="Greet Me!"/>
```

How to do it...

Add an event to `mybutton` whereby a click will fire the function `say_hello()`.

```
// original event added
$('mybutton').addEvent('click',say_hello);
```

Next, we place a trigger event on a link, suggesting to the user that the page can do more assuming that functionality is desirable to the user.

```
Hey, I wish this button would also change color on click.
<a onclick = "

    // add a new event without disturbing the existing one
    $('mybutton').addEvent('click',change_color);

" href="#">Make it change color, too.</a>
```

How it works...

When the second binding occurs, it does not disturb the original binding, allowing both actions to fire in sequence. There is not a defined, finite limit to the number of events that can be bound to the same action; although, there probably is a limit within the confines of individual client browser memory limits or perhaps even within the human memory space of us programmers.

See also

When multiple actions should be fired in a sequence in which one must complete fully before the next, or more organization is required, MooTool *Chains* can be used. The next two recipes show how to implement these chain objects.

Making one listener start a chain of events

MooTools allows us to queue up functions within an array so that each function can be called, one after the other. This is referred to as chaining. This recipe is about making a chain and then using a listener to start the chain rolling.

Getting ready

Create a small array of numbers that can be used by our script, each one made bold in sequence.

```
<div id="numbers">
    <span>1</span> <span>2</span> <span>3</span>
    <span>4</span> <span>5</span> <span>6</span> <span>7</span></div>
```

How to do it...

Define, for quick reuse, my_numbers as var my_numbers = $$('#numbers span');. Next, create a function that will advance the bold, black highlight to the next number, or start at "1" if none is active.

```
var advance_one_number = function() {
  var next_number = -1;
  my_numbers.each(function(el,index) {
    if (el.hasClass('next-in-chain')) {
      next_number = index.toInt();
    }
    el.removeClass('next-in-chain');
  });
```

```
    next_number++;
    if  ($defined(my_numbers[next_number]))  {
      my_numbers[next_number].addClass('next-in-chain');
    }
  }
}
```

It would seem that simply looping seven times and placing a delay after each call would work:
`for(i=0;i<7;i++) advance_one_number.delay(1000);`. Unfortunately, the loop
completes in a flash and all seven calls complete about 1 second later, all simultaneously.

In comes the MooTools `Chain()` class.

```
// create a chain
var my_chain = new Chain();
// record one advance into the chain for each number
my_numbers.each(function(el)  {
  my_chain.chain(advance_one_number);
});
// what to do when our button is clicked:
$('mybutton').addEvent('click',function()  {

  my_chain.callChain.delay(1000,my_chain);

});
```

How it works...

The created chain allows us to define, in an array storage format, a list of functions that are
called with each subsequent call to `Chain.callChain()`. This method also reduces the
number of chained elements as it calls the flattened, stored function.

There's more...

For those that have not yet peeked at the source code included with the book, there may be
curiosity as to where the other six calls to the chain occur. It is necessary to call the chain at
the end of the `advance_one_number` function.

```
  . . .
        my_chain.callChain.delay(1000,my_chain);
    }
```

See also

It has been said that the stand-alone `Chain` class is not meant for widespread use, that its primary purpose is to extend the chaining ability of other classes. Look at `Fx.chain()` and `Request.chain()` as some great examples of how to do that.

Removing a chain of events

Extending upon the chain of events created in the previous section, this recipe shows us how to clear a chain of events using `Chain.clearChain()`.

Getting ready

Get ready to call this function by adding a widget to which our clearing function can be bound.

```
<input type="button" id="mycancel" value="Clear Chain"/>
```

How to do it...

Calling the `clearChain()` method of the `my_chain` object, which is an instantiation of MooTools **Chain**, removes the current call stack completely.

```
$('mycancel').addEvent('click',function() {

    alert('Clearing chain:'+my_chain.$chain.length+' actions');
    my_chain.clearChain();
    alert('Done! Chain has:'+my_chain.$chain.length+' actions');

});
```

How it works...

Each call to `my_chain.chain(advance_one_number)` added another array argument to the internally maintained `$chain` array. This array is a property of the chain object instantiation. Calling `my_chain.clearChain()` zeroes out the `$chain` property of `my_chain`.

There's more...

As seen in the next screenshot, a call to `clearChain` may occur at anytime, even when some calls to the stack have already occurred:

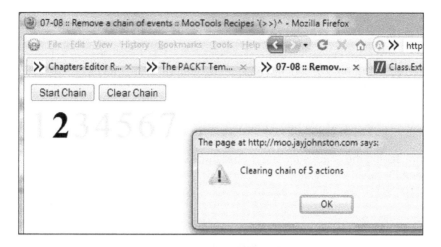

Stopping a listener from executing a chain of events

It is a feature not a bug. That jocularity may work with the right client, and using it carefully, and in the right context, may prevent a client from being angry about unexpected behavior.

Getting ready

This recipe, an extension of the last two, alters the method in which we prevent the chain from firing. Ready our receptors-of-twisted-facts to perceive the idea that a bug can be a feature.

There may be a need to stop a listener from activating a chain while still keeping the chain of events for later use.

How to do it...

Reuse the INPUT button with ID `my_cancel`, yet instead of calling the method to remove the stack of actions, Just remove the click action of the event.

```
$('mycancel').addEvent('click',function()  {

    // this removes the listener that was firing the chain
    $('mybutton').removeEvents('click');
    // but it does not remove the chain of events itself
        my_chain.callChain.delay(1000,my_chain);
        my_chain.callChain.delay(1000,my_chain);
        my_chain.callChain.delay(1000,my_chain);
    });
```

How it works...

We are very cognizant that removing the click event of `my_button` does not clear the events, as evidenced by the three, subsequent calls to `my_chain.callChain()`. These calls advance the stack three steps, shown by the bold highlighting of the number three.

There's more...

If you are not seeing the chain stop on number three, you may be starting the chain without first removing the `onClick` action of `my_button`. Click **Clear Chain** before clicking **Start Chain** to properly remove the click action.

See also

There may also be puzzlement over why clicking **Start Chain** only calls the `callChain` method once. To prevent the continued chaining of `advance_one_number` in the explanatory three calls to `callChain` in the click action bound to `my_cancel`, `//my_chain.callChain.delay(1000,my_chain);` is commented out.

But that is a feature, not a bug.

Making buttons rollover upon MOUSEOVER

Ah, the button rollover that makes navigation user friendly and fun: handling the mouseover event.

Here is a screenshot of how the buttons will look after we apply the mouseover actions:

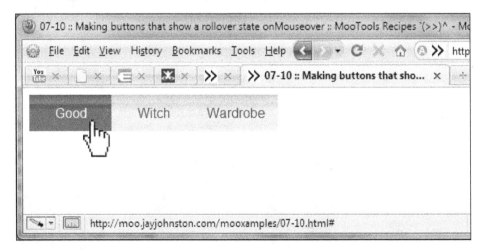

Getting ready

Mouseover effects are widely used to signal to a user that their mouse pointer has come in contact with an item that will interact with them. Get ready to create mouseover effects by creating some links. Style these links to appear as floating block buttons.

```
<a    href="#">Lion</a>
<a    href="#">Witch</a>
<a    href="#">Wardrobe</a>

<style    type="text/css">
     a    {
          display:block;    background:transparent
            url(07_button_right.gif)    no-repeat    top    right;
            width:100px;    float:left;    height:42px;
            text-align:center;    line-height:42px;
            font-family:arial;    text-decoration:none;
     }
</style>
```

How to do it...

Applying mouseover actions, *in JavaScript*, requires the use of an event listener. MooTools has a simple syntax to use for adding mouseover and mouseout actions.

```
$$('a').addEvents({
   'mouseover':function()    {
      this.setStyles({
         'color':'#FFF',
         'background-position':'bottom'
      });
      this.set('text',text_changer(this.get('text')));
   },
   'mouseout':function()    {
      this.setStyles({
         'color':'#00F',
         'background-position':'top'
      });
      this.set('text',text_changer(this.get('text')));
   }
});
```

The collection of A tag elements, `$$('a')`, has event listeners assigned to it via the MooTools `Element.addEvents()` object. The mandatory parameter is an object that defines a hash of definable actions along with their bound functions.

How it works...

The bound function for the event `mouseover` looks like this:

```
function()  {
    this.setStyles({
      'color':'#FFF',
      'background-position':'bottom'
    });
    this.set('text',text_changer(this.get('text')));
  }
```

Though the style change could be handled by the CSS pseudo-class `:hover`, the change of the button text can only be accomplished using JavaScript. With the assistance of a helper function, `text_changer()`, we use MooTools' `Element.get()` to get the inner text and then `Element.set()` to set the new text value.

There's more

The slightly less used `switch` statement construct, which has a more concise syntax than nested if/else blocks, is not a MooTools function. It is raw JavaScript and found in most languages like Perl, PHP, Bash, and many others including ActionScript.

Changing graphics upon MOUSEOVER

Many corporate websites make use of this content-changing mechanism to bring a new level of professionalism to their front pages.

Getting ready

Launching off our previous recipe, we add a new level of interaction. Prepare both the mouseover and mouseout `Element.addEvents()` code blocks, as well as three images to use for the new DOM element that will be updated when our button listeners are fired. This screenshot shows how the lady figurine appears when the **Witch** button is moused over:

How to do it...

The mouseover action is adjusted with a new line of code that uses the button/image naming structure to update the background style properties of the DOM element `pic`.

```
. . .
        'mouseover':function()  {
            this.setStyles({'color':'#FFF',
                'background-position':'bottom'});
            var  txt  =  this.get('text');
            this.set('text',text_changer(txt));
            $('pic').setStyle('background','#FFF  url(07_'+txt+'.jpg)
                no-repeat  top  left');
        },
. . .
```

How it works...

The mouseover action allows the use of the `this` keyword. That does not prevent us from making actions upon seemingly unrelated DOM elements. The DIV `pic` is innocently standing by and unaware (from a DOM perspective) of the actions happening upon mouseover and mouseout of the buttons. Using `Element.setStyle()`, we effortlessly update the background to have the appropriate picture.

 Note that on mouseout we use `Element.setStyle()` to then remove the picture from the DOM. This may change based on personal preference or client requirements. In many cases, having the image remain is preferred behavior.

Using MooTools Fx in conjunction with onmouseover events

Mouseover actions are great and when combined with smooth effects, most users cannot distinguish them from flash objects.

Getting ready

The previous two recipes have prepared us to add effects to our mouseover, button-shows-image creation. After reviewing those two concepts of attaching the event listeners and altering unrelated DOM elements, we are ready to make the images appear in a milky smooth, moo-fashion.

How to do it...

Rather than making the images suddenly show up, we instantiate a moo-effect upon the DIV pic. Using that effect object, we fade in and out the opacity of the DIV as the images are added and removed.

```
$$('a').addEvents({
  'mouseover':function()  {

      // if the pic is visible, hide it fast
      $('pic').fade('hide');

      this.setStyles({'color':'#FFF','background-position':'bottom'});
      var  txt  =  this.get('text');
      this.set('text',text_changer(txt));
      $('pic').setStyle('background','#FFF  url(07_'+txt+'.jpg)  no-
repeat  top  left');

      // the background is set...fade it in using Fx.Tween
      $('pic').fade('in');

  },
  'mouseout':function()  {
      this.setStyles({'color':'#00F','background-position':'top'});
      this.set('text',text_changer(this.get('text')));

      // fade out the pic before removing it
      $('pic').fade('out');

  }
});
```

How it works...

The **Fx** class is part of the extension MooTools provides to DOM elements collected using `$()` and `$$()`. It extends the elements with the methods `Element.tween()`, `Element.highlight()`, and as demonstrated here, `Element.fade()`.

Fx/Fx.Tween

Making use of the Element Custom Types of the **Fx** class can save many lines of code. Be sure to read what methods each class infuses into DOM elements before instantiating a MooTools class to act upon elements that already have the ability to do the desired action or effect.

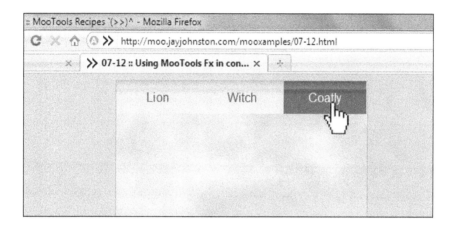

See also

The `Fx` transition used in this recipe is just the tip of that *cold*, proverbial iceberg. Look into the juicy stuff in *Chapter 8, Dynamite! (Movin' On Up): Working with Transitions*, and begin transitioning your websites with some rather slick eye candy!

8

Dynamite! (Movin' On Up): Working with Transitions

Slide it, fade it, animate it, move it, bump it, make it bounce, make it stretch, and go *boi-oi-oi-ng*. That is just a little preview of what MooTools does like no other framework can. Other frameworks even use MooTools' code to handle their tweens and morphs.

By way of a segue (transition) to the chapter itself, you will find in this chapter:

- ▶ Transitioning sizes of DOM elements with Fx.Morph
- ▶ Sliding text around with Fx.Slide
- ▶ Animation, fade-ificaion, and tool tips

Saving space on our site: expanding upon interaction

Has our client said the "above-the-fold" phrase again? Here is an example on how to get more above the fold, while still allowing for the text entry box with which to send those glowing comments about how usable our site is.

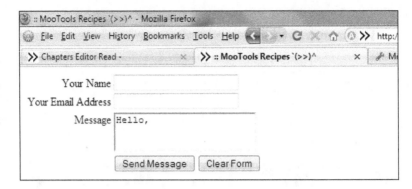

See in this second image how the focused box expands smoothly and fades to yellow:

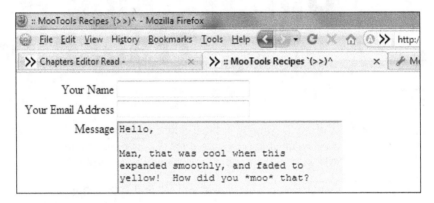

Getting ready

Once our form is created, we append an ID attribute to the target TEXTAREA element to make single dollar collection of the element easier when we write our MooScript.

```
<textarea
    id="grow-grow-grow"
    style="width:200px;height:50px;"
    name="customer_comments">
Hello,
</textarea>
```

While using ID attributes and single dollar concatenation may always seem fastest, we are always on the lookout for ways to reduce the amount of code a search engine has to read through. In this case, the ID collection seems the best choice, like this: $ ('<ID>'). A swarm of nested elements like list items in an UL would call for $$ ('#<ID> li') and offer us the opportunity to loop over the elements.

Using multiple frameworks? Have the time-tested and faithful, single dollar set aside for use by other frameworks and used the newly created document.id() in the same way the once ubiquitous $() was used.

How to do it...

Use the single dollar object $(), or document.id() to add two event listeners, as we did in the previous chapter on listeners.

```
$('grow-grow-grow').addEvents({
  'focus':function() {
    this.morph({
      'width':'300px',
      'height':'200px',
      'background-color':'#FFF79F'
    });
  },
  'blur':function() {
    this.morph({
      'width':'200px',
      'height':'50px',
      'background-color':'#FFFFFF'
    });
  }
});
```

How it works...

The MooTools class Fx.Morph is usable as an Element property. Call Element.morph() to make use of this method. The morphing object will transition from the current style(s) property to the requested property.

`Fx.Tween`, which transitions only one single style property, and `Fx.Morph`, which will transition multiple properties simultaneously, both also accept an alternative, two-element array construct for the style property value. Passing the start and end values in this way will ignore the current style value of the element.

```
. . .
    this.morph({
        'width':[300,200],
        'height':[100,50],
        'background-color':['#FFF79F','#FFFFFF']
    });
. . .
```

Saving space on our site: creating a transition that grows an IMG from small to large

In this recipe we will learn about how to use the mouse over an image technique to enlarge the image.

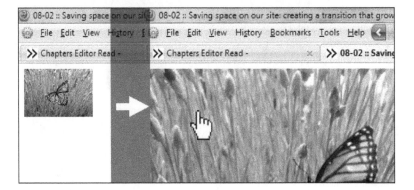

Getting ready

Prepare a thumbnail image that is constrained via a CSS class definition, `.smaller_image`.

```
<img src="08_nature.jpg" alt="Nature" class="smaller_img"/>

<style type="text/css">
  .smaller_img { width:100px; }
  .bigger_img { width:500px; }
</style>
```

How to do it...

Much like the previous recipe, we use the MooTooled element property, which comes from the `Fx.Morph()` class. The difference in this recipe is that we pass to `Element.morph()` the class that contains the style definition to transition to.

```
$$('img').addEvents({
  'mouseover':function() {
    this.morph('.bigger_img');
  },
  'mouseout':function() {
    this.morph('.smaller_img');
  }
});
```

How it works...

Once the `mouseover` and `mouseout` events are added by the `Element.addEvents()` construct, each event calls the assigned morph and passes the assigned class.

> The class, itself, is not actually added to the element's class attribute. The class style definition is used to dynamically alter the DOM using inline CSS:
> `<img class="smaller_img" alt="Nature picture" src="08_nature.jpg" style="width: 500px;">`.

Saving space on our site: the "more" button that shows more with a transition

The "more" link is a frequently used space saver. *More* frequently than not, it links to another page with a clunky HTTP refresh. In this recipe, we see how to save the space and keep the data on the page, **for both the search engines and our users**.

Getting ready

We start with an outer DIV that hides overflow and has styles that limit the height. Putting the actual text within an inner DIV will allow us to pick up the natural, auto-height of the element based on its text.

```
<style type="text/css">
  .news_outer { height:40px; width:400px; overflow:hidden; }
  ...
```

How to do it...

Set a listener on the DIV, which starts out as reading **More** on screen. Toggle that text to and from "Less" and the height of the outer DIV based on the initialized height of the outer element. This initial height must match that used in the style `.news_outer`.

```
var news_outer_ht = 40;
$$('.more_news').addEvent('click',function() {
  var el = this.getPrevious('.news_outer');
  var outer_ht = el.getStyle('height').toInt();
  var inner_ht = el.getChildren('.news_inner')[0].
    getStyle('height').toInt();
  if (outer_ht==news_outer_ht) {
    var new_ht = inner_ht;
    var txt = 'Less';
  } else {
    var new_ht = news_outer_ht;
    var txt = 'More';
  }
  el.tween('height',new_ht);
  this.set('text',txt);
});
```

How it works...

To get the height that the outer DIV should grow to, `inner_ht`, we pick up our outer news DIV, `el` by first traversing the DOM from our clicked, *More/Less* DIV to the first previous sibling of `this` that has the class `news_outer` and then traversing to the first child of `el`.

There's more...

Fx.Morph versus Fx.Tween

The term "Tween", as it pertains to MooTools > 1.2, indicates that a single CSS property will be transitioned. To transition multiple style properties, use *Morph* which requires the object syntax instead of the two-argument syntax required by `Element.tween()`.

The MooTools documentation for `Element.Tween` shows several syntax options: `http://mootools.net/docs/core/Fx/Fx.Tween#Element:tween`. Another way to handle this type of space saving is with the MooTools More Accordion: `http://mootools.net/demos/?demo=Accordion`, though, unlike the solution in this recipe, the page will load initially with all accordion nodes expanded.

Saving space on our site: expand text containers on focus

Continuing in our effort to save space, we will endeavor to expand text containers on focus.

Getting ready

Prepare our DOM for this recipe where each text field greets the focus from the user by expanding smoothly, create regular `INPUT` elements. The code snippet in the book also includes a `TEXTAREA`. Also define two states of CSS to represent both blurred and focused elements.

```
...
<tr>
<td align="right"><label for="name">Your Name</label></td>
  <td><input type="text" value="" name="name" id="name"></td>
</tr>
<tr>
<td align="right">
  <label for="email">Your Email Address</label>
</td>
  <td>
   <input type="text" value="" name="email" id="email">
</td>
</tr>
...
  <style type="text/css">
    .blurred_element {
     width:100px; background-color:#FFFFFF;
   }
    .focused_element {
     width:300px; background-color:#FFF79F;
   }
  </style>
```

How to do it...

Attach listeners to `onBlur` and `onFocus` that will execute `Element.morph` and pass the appropriate class to transition to.

```
$$('input[type=text],textarea').each(function(el) {
  el.addClass('blurred_element');
  el.addEvents({
    'focus':function() {
      this.morph('.focused_element');
    },
    'blur':function() {
      this.morph('.blurred_element');
    }
  });
});
```

How it works...

As the user tabs into, or mouse-clicks into one of the fields with listeners attached, the field grows. When the user tabs out of, or mouse-clicks out of the field, it returns to the blurred state.

Welcoming users in a flashy way: flying in text smoothly

In *Chapter 4, That's Not All Folks: Animation and Scrolling*, using MooTools More, we slid in text using `Fx.Slide`. This recipe shows how to slide in text with only the MooTools Core and not the More.

Getting ready

Plan the final size and destination of the message and nest it within a parent element that can hold the position while the message is moved absolutely in the DOM. Position the flying DIV absolutely and off to the top left of the page.

```
<div id="main">
  <div id="place_holder">
    <div id="flying_div">Hooray, you are here!</div>
  </div>
</div>

<style type="text/css">
#main { width:600px;  margin:auto; }
#place_holder {
  margin:auto;
  width:300px;
  height:100px;
}
#flying_div {
  width:300px;
  line-height:100px;
  font-size:25px;
  text-align:center;
}
</style>
```

How to do it...

Use `Element.getPosition()` to pick up the x and y values of the parent, placeholder DIV. Pass those values to `Element.morph()` to transition the absolute positioning, smoothly flying the message DIV into its relatively positioned parent.

```
window.addEvent('load',function() {
  var new_pos = $('place_holder').getPosition();
  $('flying_div').morph({
    'opacity':[0-1],
    'left':new_pos.x,
    'top':new_pos.y
  });
});
```

How it works...

Once the page has loaded, the `onLoad` event of the window triggers the `Element.morph()` which is programmed to fly into the coordinates of the placeholder DIV.

There's more...

Using `'opacity':[0-1]` in our morphing property argument allows us to also transition the opacity property of our object from completely transparent to completely opaque.

See also

The effect happens so fast, some users may miss it. See the next recipe, which shows how to slow down the transition and change it from a linear transition to a bouncy transition.

Welcoming users in a flashy way: stretchy elastic

Here we will learn to use fly-in text that bounces into place with a stretchy, elastic feel to it.

Getting ready

Prepare by using the same HTML markup as the previous recipe.

How to do it...

In the previous recipe, using `Fx.morph` via the enhanced element properties like this, `Element.morph()` gave us a simple way of morphing multiple-style properties. Add the optional secondary argument to the method to alter the `duration` and `transition` type.

```
window.addEvent('load',function() {
  var options = {
    duration: 5000,
    transition: 'elastic:out'
  }
  $('flying_div').set('morph',options);
  var new_pos = $('place_holder').getPosition();
  $('flying_div').morph({
    'opacity':[0,1],
    'left':new_pos.x,
    'top':new_pos.y
  });
});
```

How it works...

We are familiar with how `Element.set()` allows us to set the properties of a DOM element, properties like `HREF`, `SRC`, and `HTML`. Since all elements are extended with the `Fx.morph`, `Fx.fade`, and `Fx.highlight` properties, these object properties can be altered using the same setter method.

There's more...

Note that it is not possible to pass the options as a secondary argument to `Element.morph()`. That method always expects a single, mandatory argument that is either a string, CSS class to morph to, or an object of key-value pairs, style properties, and their values.

See also

The available transition types are numerous, including `linear`, `bounce`, and `elastic` and can be made to calculate the easing of a transition both at the beginning, `:in`, the end, `:out` or both start and end `:elastic:in:out`. Read about those and how to create our own custom transitions at `http://mootools.net/docs/core/Fx/Fx.Transitions`.

Making a little duck bounce when clicked

This is arguably useful at best, but, goodness gracious, it is goobly goblets of fun!

Getting ready

Position the standing and bouncing versions of our duck, stacked in absolute positioning so that the standing version obscures the bouncing version.

```
<div id="main">
  <div id="duck_it">
    <img src="08_duck_bounce.jpg" alt="Ouch!"
         title="Ouch!" id="bounce"/>
    <img src="08_duck_stand.jpg" alt="Click me!"
         title="Click me!" id="stand"/>
  </div>
</div>

<style type="text/css">
#main { width:600px;  margin:auto; }
#duck_it { margin-top:10px; cursor:pointer; }
#duck_it img { position:absolute; }
</style>
```

How to do it...

The last recipe made brief notice of another **Fx** property of the Element class. Within the `onStart` and `onComplete` options of `Element.tween`, use `Element.fade()`, passing it the proper keyword to immediately show or hide the appropriate image.

> The special methods `onStart` and `onComplete` allow us to be very creative about making other related (or unrelated) actions occur when our effects start up or complete. Several examples of how `onComplete` empowers our tandem-action options are shown in this chapter. Try adding something creative to the base recipes using `onStart` to earn the next level belt!

```
$('duck_it').set('tween',{
  property: 'margin-top',
  transition: 'bounce:out',
  duration: 'short',
  onStart: function() {
    $('stand').fade('hide');
    $('bounce').fade('show');
  },
  onComplete: function() {
    $('bounce').fade('hide');
    $('stand').fade('show');
```

```
    }
  }).addEvent('click',function() {
    this.tween(-100,10);
  });
```

Meanwhile, the click action is *tweening* the top margin style property and transitioning the end of the easing with a bouncy effect.

There's more...

Luke clamors, *"Hey, what's with that* blah_blah_blah().addEvent() *syntax anyway??"*
Yoda responds, *"Return* this *from every method, and object chaining you shall have."*

 Most MooTool methods return the keyword this so that they can be dot-concatenated to the next method to call. Careful use of this can make code more concise. Brazen use of this can make code more difficult to maintain.

See also

In our example, we chain together methods for a single object; however, Sean McArthur discusses how chaining methods together can cause loop-overhead on collections: http://mootools.net/blog/2010/03/19/a-better-way-to-use-elements/.

Showing a notification to a user that glows momentarily

Usability means making interfaces that really speak to users; speak volumes by getting their attention.

Getting ready

Whenever we are getting ready to introduce elements that move or grow or appear or disappear, we always take into consideration non-sighted users. Be ready for disabled users.

How to do it...

Prepare a form element that has a message that follows the element in the DOM. Any error message can be written there, perhaps some message regarding validation of the element. Let us just whimsically play a name game to demonstrate.

```
<form action="" method="get">
  <label for="name">Name: </label>
  <input type="text" name="name" value=""/>
  <span id="error_message"></span>
  <br/>
  <input type="button" value="submit"/>
</form>
```

How it works...

Each time a key is released within the form element, a bound function calls an effect that is chained to glow smoothly in and smoothly out. Each successive call to the function is itself also chained causing two levels of chaining.

```
var e = $('error_message');
var myfx = new Fx.Tween(e,{
  property:'backgroundColor',
  duration:1000,
  link:'chain'
});
$$('form input[type=text]').addEvent('keyup',function() {
  // set the error message text
  e.set('text',
    'Hey!  My name is '+this.get('value')+' too!');
  // make it glow
  myfx.start('#FF0').chain(function() {
    this.start('#FFF');
  });
});
```

There's more...

The `Fx.Tween` and `Fx.Morph` classes are intended for use within other classes. Here is an example of how to the same effect from within the more accessible and extended `Element.tween` construct.

```
<form action="" method="get">
  <label for="name">Name:</label>
  <input type="text" name="name" value="John Jaccob Jingleheimer"/>
  <span id="error_message"></span>
```

```
</form>

<script type="text/javascript">
var e = $('error_message');
e.set('text', 'Hey!  My name is John Jaccob Jingleheimer, too!');
e.set('tween',{link:'chain',property:'background-color'});
for (i=0;i<10;i++) e.tween('#FF0').tween('#FFF');
</script>
```

See also

John Jacob Jingleheimer Schmidt, a song one author's mother sang with him at the top of their lungs in joyous revelry, totally inspired this recipe: `http://en.wikipedia.org/wiki/John_Jacob_Jingleheimer_Schmidt`.

Making a golf ball ease up to a hole and stop

Using transitions to animate image movement on the screen is great fun—and, it works on the iPhone.

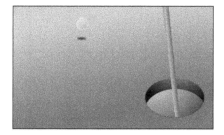

Getting ready

Prepare three images: the golf green, the golf ball, and the golf ball's shadow.

```
<div id="green"></div>

<style type="text/css">
#green {
  margin:0 auto;
  background:transparent url('08_golf_green.jpg') no-repeat 0 0;
  width:500px; height:500px;
}
</style>
```

```
<script type="text/javascript">
// inject the ball
var ball = new Element('img',{
  id: 'ball',
  src: '08_golf_ball.png',
  style: 'width:10px; position:absolute;',
  morph: {
    link:'chain',
    transition:'linear'
  }
}).inject('green','top');

// inject the ball's shadow
var shad = new Element('img',{
...

alert('Ready?');
```

We also need the movement coordinates of the ball.

```
// top, left, width
var ballmov = [
  [150, 10, 10],
  [ 20, 20, 10], // bounce 1
  [160, 30, 10],
  [100, 40, 10], // bounce 2
  [180, 50, 15],
  [140, 75, 20], // bounce 3
  [220,100, 25],
  [200,150, 30], // bounce 4
  [300,200, 40],
  [400,250, 50], // basically rolling now
  [420,300, 60]
];
```

How to do it...

Use chained calls to an `Fx.Morph()` instance to move the ball along the green, growing it slightly as it rolls and bounces along.

```
var shad_bottom = 150;
ballmov.each(function(el,i) {
  var extra = (el[2]/4).toInt();
  if (el[0]>shad_bottom) shad_bottom = el[0]+extra;
  else shad_bottom*=1.03;
```

```
    //shad_bottom = el[0]+extra;
    $('ball').morph({
      'margin-top':el[0],
      'margin-left':el[1],
      'width':el[2]
    });
    $('shad').morph({
      'margin-top':shad_bottom,
      'margin-left':el[1],
      'width':el[2]
    });
  });
```

How it works...

Once we have set the `link` property of `Element.morph()`, multiple calls will be chained together. Looping over the coordinate values of `ballmov`, we set the morph calls to transition the position of the ball, chaining together each movement towards the hole.

There's more...

Changing the graphics to, say, make the ball a grasshopper and the shadow of a bug the grasshopper is chasing, alter the transition to `quart:in:out` and see how the different transition effects can make a set of code applicable to multiple animation scenarios.

Making usability cool with fading font-size changer

There are many different ways to change fonts on a page. Using MooTools allows us a fancy variety of options. Use morphing to smoothly transition from one text size to the next.

Getting ready

To be ready to transition font size, the layout must be liquid. A *liquid layout* is one that can grow without breaking the display. Create styles that would alter the size of the text.

```
<div id="main" class="medium">
<form action="" method="get" id="font_sizer">
  Choose text size:
  <input type="button" id="small" value="S"/>
  <input type="button" id="medium" value="M"
    disabled="disabled"/>
  <input type="button" id="large" value="L"/>
```

```
        </form>
        <h1>Welcome!</h1>
<p>
Lorem ipsum dolor sit amet, consectetur adipiscing elit. Donec nec
auctor est. Aenean neque sem, vulputate quis ultrices quis...etc,
homma homma.
...
      </div>

    <style type="text/css">
      #main {  margin:0 auto; width:780px; padding:10px; }

      .small { font-size:10px; }
      .medium { font-size:14px; }
      .large { font-size:20px; }
    </style>
```

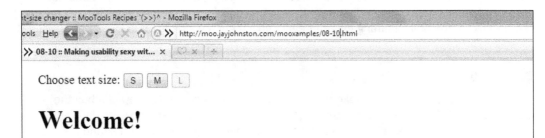

How to do it...

Use the INPUT buttons to determine which class to switch to and call Element.morph(), passing it the proper new class to morph to.

```
    var ibuttons = $$('#font_sizer input[type=button]');
    ibuttons.addEvent('click',function() {
      var newsize = this.get('id');
      ibuttons.removeProperty('disabled');
      $(newsize).set('disabled','disabled');
      $('main').morph('.'+newsize);
    });
```

How it works...

Notable in Firefox's Firebug HTML panel, the class associated with #main remains as "medium" throughout the script. This is an initialization of the presentation layer. When the morph occurs, an inline style is altering the presentation layer, overriding the class: hence the term, **C**ascading **S**tyle **S**heets (CSS).

There's more...

An element has many properties. Use `Element.removeProperty()` to remove attribute tags like ID, SRC, HREF, CHECKED, DISABLED as well as other properties assigned to any given element in the DOM.

Fading through a rotating group of images—slideshow!

Typically, it seems, the DOM markup for a slideshow is harrowing. This example will show how that markup can be made much more straightforward.

Getting ready

Ready our DOM with a simple, unimposing markup. To allow the page to gracefully degrade in the absence of JavaScript, place the initial image as the background of #fodaddy.

```
<div id="fodaddy">
  <div id="fo"></div>
</div>

<style type="text/css">
#fodaddy {
  width:367px;
  background-image:url('08_cow_one.jpg');
}
#fo, #fodaddy {
  height:318px;
}
</style>
```

How to do it...

Inject the main, viewable image behind #fo and set #fo to a zero opacity so that it is invisible, allowing the main image to be the only item seen by users. Place a new image in #fo, which is our *curtain* of sorts, and then *pull the curtain* on the main image by fading in a bit of *fo*; then repeat endlessly in a loop.

Identify which images to loop through. Remember that the image in the first position, images[0], should already be set as the background of #fodaddy.

```
var images = [
'08_cow_one.jpg',
'08_cow_two.jpg',
'08_cow_three.jpg',
];
```

The speed of the transition and the delay between transitions is measured in milliseconds. Variable mynext has global scope to track which image we are working with.

```
var ispeed = 2000;
var mynext = 1;
```

Setting the morph properties of element #fo allows us to control the morph and fire an action upon completion.

```
$('fo').set('morph', {
  link: 'chain',
  duration: ispeed,
  // after the curtain pulls, switch it all up!
  onComplete: function() {
    $('fosure').fade('in');
    $('fosure').set('src',images[mynext]);
    mynext = (++mynext>=images.length) ? 0 : mynext;
    //setTimeout('changeImage()',ispeed);
    change_image.delay(ispeed);
  }
});
```

Use a utility function to fade in the "curtain".

```
var change_image = function() {
  $('fo').fade(
    'hide'
  ).setStyle(
    'background-image',
    'url('+images[mynext]+')'
  ).morph({'opacity':1});
}
```

Of course, it is necessary to set the ball in motion so that our slideshow can begin upon page load. This is where #fosure, the main image, is injected into the DOM.

```
window.addEvent('load',function() {
  var fosure = new Element('img',{
    'id': 'fosure',
    'src': images[1],
    'style': 'position:absolute;'
  }).inject('fodaddy','top').fade('hide');
  change_image.delay(ispeed);
  //setTimeout('changeImage()',ispeed);
});
```

There's more...

Here is a capture of how the image rotation and *curtain pulling* looks both on the screen and within Firefox's Firebug plugin.

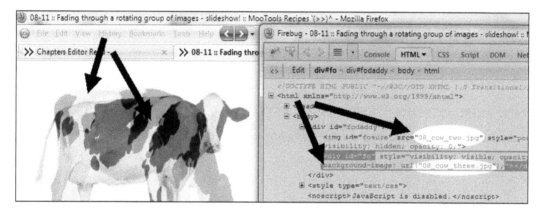

9
WTFudge is Going On?: Troubleshooting MooTools

It is impossible to change and fill one's automobile oil (with any precision) without a dipstick.

And we all know that running LAN cable is much easier when there is a cable tester pair handy.

Should we throw out that battery? A battery or lead tester is invaluable.

Tools of the trade always include items for troubleshooting. JavaScript errors, DOM manipulation, and Ajax calls are no different: the tools we use to debug during development make or break us.

Flip through this chapter to see ideas on how to:

- ▶ Troubleshoot using debug consoles in Firefox and IE
- ▶ View the members of non-scalar values
- ▶ Watch the seemingly intangible traffic of Ajax calls

Using Firefox's Firebug to see MooTool stuff in action

Knowing how to see what has changed on the page is paramount; **View | Source** will not help us. The source that is displayed by any browser (**View | Page Source** in Firefox), is loaded only once when the page is requested. Any changes we make dynamically to the Document Object Model (DOM) are tracked by the DOM but the original page source itself is not updated.

Getting ready

Download the Firefox "Add-on", Firebug. This option is available from the Tools menu in Firefox. Search for "Firebug" and download the add-on, install it, and restart the browser.

How to do it...

1. Create a test page using the code below.
2. Right-click the DIV #canvas. Be sure to click the words that make up the HTML of the DIV: **Right click here and choose "Inspect Element"**. Right-clicking the HTML of that DIV tells Firebug which element in the DOM to inspect.
3. While watching the Firebug HTML panel, click #go represented by the text **Once Firebug is inspecting the DOM, click here!**.

Generate an error by clicking **Now see an error in Firebug**.

In the bottom right of Firebug, there is an emboldened, red x with a message stating how many errors have occurred: for example, **(X) 1 Error**; click that to automatically open the Firebug Console panel to view the error.

 In this example, the undefined_function() call was *purposefully* called without first creating the function to demonstrate how to view errors in Firebug.

```
<div id="canvas">
  Right click here and choose "Inspect Element"
</div>
<a href="#" id="go">
  Once Firebug is inspecting the DOM, click here!
</a>
<a href="#" id="error">
  Now see an error in Firebug
</a>
```

```
<script type="text/javascript">
  $('go').addEvent('click',function() {
  var html = '<strong>Hello <em>World</em>!</strong>';
    $('canvas').set('html',html);
  });
  $('error').addEvent('click',function() {
    undefined_function();
  });
</script>
```

How it works...

Firebug has added to the contextual, right-click menu of Firefox. The addition of **Inspect Element** in that menu gives us the ability to take a direct shortcut to the element that we wish to inspect.

When ID #go is clicked, a function bound to that element's click event changes the contents of #canvas. Though we cannot see this if we **View | Source**, it is visible in Firebug:

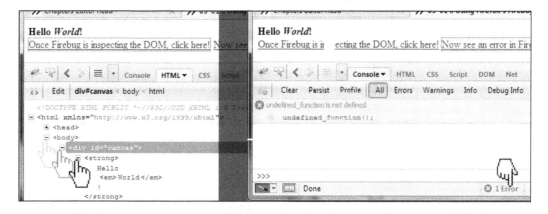

It seems odd to create an error on purpose; yet, in this example, we do so in order to prepare our debugging muscle memory for those unexpected errors. Launch the Firebug Console panel to review errors by clicking the bold, red "Error". That bold, red message appears in our recipe after clicking #error in our DOM attempts to call the *purposefully* undefined function.

There's more...

Cascading Style Sheets (CSS) can make troubleshooting where styles are coming from feel like dancing with a porcupine. While the Firebug HTML panel is open, click directly on any of the tags, (**click on** `<div` **rather than on the inner portion of the tag**). To the right of the HTML, in a default Firebug layout, the CSS panel shows how an element's CSS has been created, where it is cascading from, and what declarations are overridden (by using *strike* to display the overridden properties).

See also

Watch a video by Jim Plush on editing CSS in Firebug to get used to how the various panels interact `http://www.youtube.com/watch?v=FsX6qwQqGgQ`.

Using IE's Developer Toolbar to see MooTool stuff in action

We can use nearly the same DOM example as the last recipe. There are a few extra comments since IE forgets what element we are inspecting.

Getting ready

To get the IE Developer Toolbar, go into **Internet Options | Programs** (tab) | **Manage add-ons** (button). Find the IE Developer Toolbar under **Microsoft Windows Component Publisher** and be sure it is enabled.

How to do it...

1. Finding anything in IE is a bear. Keep our sanity by using keyboard shortcuts. On the keyboard press the *F12* key to open the debugger.

2. To select the `#canvas` DIV, press *Ctrl+B* to put IE Developer Toolbar in an odd, mouseover mode.

3. Mouseover the `#canvas` DIV and click once.

4. The HTML panel in IE Developer Toolbar opens and the `#canvas` DIV is selected; expand it by clicking the plus sign.

5. Watching the panel is useless since any change in DOM must be completely reloaded in the toolbar. Click **Now that the Developer Toolbar is showing #canvas, click here!**.

6. To see how the DOM has changed, redo the first few steps to reopen the toolbar panel to the `#canvas` DIV.

7. Generate an error by clicking **Now see an error in IE**.

8. In the bottom left of IE, there is probably a small yellow caution symbol next to the words **Error on page**; clicking that likely does little, dependent on what other software is installed.

9. To view the error and offending code, press to open the debugger toolbar, select the **Script** panel, and then select the **Console** button in the top of the right pane.

How it works...

Once the debugger toolbar is open and the `#canvas` DOM element is being inspected (after applying the DOM change enacted by clicking `#go`), the toolbar and website display as shown:

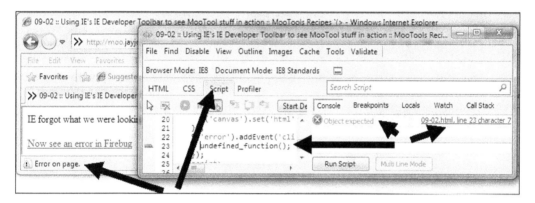

Reviewing the error message should show a configuration similar to the following composite image:

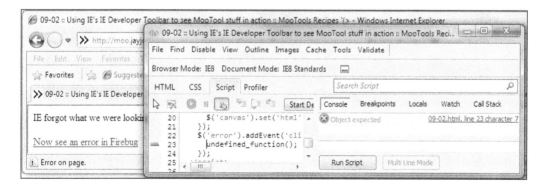

There's more...

A powerful method of stepping through client-side code is available for free. Downloading the Microsoft Script Debugger and activating it will cause any error to prompt the user/developer as to whether they would like to debug the script that has errored. Launching the debugger, which comes standard with Visual Studio.net, allows for the exact variable stack and call order to be reviewed.

See also

The Microsoft Developer Network (MSDN) blog has an article on where to go next
`http://blogs.msdn.com/b/ie/archive/2004/10/26/247912.aspx.`

Reporting the type of a variable

Objects and variables get confusing; save a few moments by making them report to us.

Getting ready

To test a battery of variables, one must instantiate a battery of variables.

```
// string variable, integer, array, object, null, undefined
  var string_var = 'hello';
  var integer_var = 1972;
  var array_var = ['1','two',3];
  var object_var = {one: '1', two: 'two', three: function() {
    alert(3); }}
  var null_var;
  //var oops_var; // commented out "on purpose"
```

How to do it...

Call a function that reports the type of each of our variables.

```
<h2>without moo:</h2>
  <script type="text/javascript">
    report_typeOf(0);
  </script>

  <h2><strong>with</strong> moo:</h2>
  <script type="text/javascript">
    report_typeOf(1);
  </script>
```

How it works...

The raw JavaScript "type of" function, which is built-in and requires no function construct, uses a lower case "O": typeof(). **The MooTools version** of this attempts to fix the deficiencies in the rushed-to-market version of typeof and uses an upper case "O": typeOf().

```
function report_typeOf(ismoo) {
  if (ismoo==0) {
    document.write('string: '+typeof(string_var)+'<br/>');
    document.write('integer: '+typeof(integer_var)+'<br/>');
    document.write('<strong>array:
      '+typeof(array_var)+'</strong><br/>');
    document.write('object: '+typeof(object_var)+'<br/>');
    document.write('object: '+typeof(object_var.three)+'<br/>');
    document.write('<strong>null:
      '+typeof(null_var)+'</strong><br/><br/>');
    document.write('undefined: '+typeof(oops_var)+'<br/>');
  } else {
    document.write('string: '+typeOf(string_var)+'<br/>');
    document.write('integer: '+typeOf(integer_var)+'<br/>');
    document.write('array: '+typeOf(array_var)+'<br/>');
    document.write('object: '+typeOf(object_var)+'<br/>');
    document.write('object: '+typeOf(object_var.three)+'<br/>');
    document.write('null: '+typeOf(null_var)+'<br/><br/>');
    // oddity with 1.3.0 typeOf and undefined:
    document.write('undefined: '+((typeof(oops_var)==
      'undefined')?':(':typeOf(oops_var)+'<br/>'));
    document.write('undefined: '+typeOf(oops_var)+'<br/>');
    // in chapter 10, we create extend typeOf to patch this behavior
  }
}
```

There's more...

There is an oddity of sorts with sending undefined variables to typeOf. As of version 1.3.1, the oddity still exists, and it is worth our time to check this in future releases as the documentation suggests that **undefined, null, NaN or none of the above** return "null".

> Meanwhile, a somewhat unfortunate call to typeof(myvar) may be warranted in complex applications where variable scoping may render a potentially usable variable undefined, causing Moo to error out within typeOf.

See also

Read about why raw JavaScript needs to have some functions extended in this way at `http://javascript.crockford.com/remedial.html`.

Determining the browser version of a visitor

MooTools is cross-browser compliant, but CSS is not always as nice; let's figure out what browser is visiting us.

How to do it...

Create a string that has browser and platform particulars in it.

```
var browser_info = 'Your browser info: '+
    Browser.name+' '+
    Browser.version+' on '+
    Browser.Platform.name;
```

How it works...

MooTools works regular expression magic on the `navigator.userAgent`. See this snippet from the source:

```
var ua = navigator.userAgent.toLowerCase(),
  platform = navigator.platform.toLowerCase(),
  UA = ua.match(/(opera|ie|firefox|chrome|version)[s/:]([wd.]+)?.*?(
    safari|version[s/:]([wd.]+)|$)/) || [null, 'unknown', 0],
  mode = UA[1] == 'ie' && document.documentMode;

var Browser = this.Browser = {
  extend: Function.prototype.extend,
  name: (UA[1] == 'version') ? UA[3] : UA[1],
  version: mode || parseFloat((UA[1] == 'opera' && UA[4]) ?
    UA[4] : UA[2]),
  Platform: {
    name: ua.match(/ip(?:ad|od|hone)/) ? 'ios' : (ua.match(
      /(?:webos|android)/) || platform.match(/mac|win|linux/)
      || ['other'])[0]
  },
  ...
```

There's more...

Using the following Boolean values can also be helpful: `Browser.firefox`, `Browser.chrome`, `Browser.safari`, and `Browser.opera`.

See also

To get a list of the Boolean values that show available features and plugins, for instance `Browser.Features.json` and `Browser.Plugins.Flash`, browse over to `http://mootools.net/docs/core/Browser/Browser#Browser:Browser-Features` and `http://mootools.net/docs/core/Browser/Browser#Browser:Browser-Plugins`.

Using Firebug to view the scripts included on a page

Firebug is the best way to catch our JavaScript errors; it can also give us short cuts to seeing the included JavaScript files.

Getting ready

Open a page that has one or more JavaScript files included via SCRIPT tags. The code snippets in the book include one for just this purpose, though, any of them will do.

How to do it...

Open the Firebug window and click the **Script** tab. The horizontal bar beneath the tab list will have a drop-down that shows the name of the URI, for instance, **09-05.html**. This drop-down menu will have a list of each script that is included. Visible in the list, if viewing the scripts for 09-05.html, will be **09-05.html**, **mootools-1.3.0.js**, and **mootools-more-1.3.0.js**.

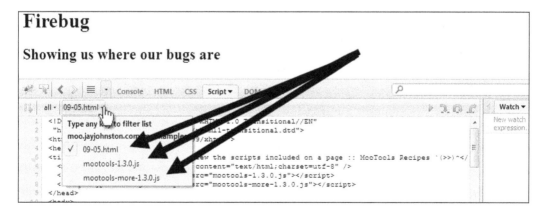

Clicking on any of these files will load the source into the panel for review.

There's more

The scripts panel allows us to do a lot more than just review static sources. This full-power debugger lets us interact with scripts. Clicking on the line numbers sets *breakpoints*. Reload to have the script pause at each breakpoint, and use the debugging controls Continue (*F8*), Step Into (*F11*), Step Over (*F10*), and Step Out (*Shift+F11*) to step through the scripts.

 Conditional breakpoints can be created by right-clicking the line-numbers. Place an expression that will cause the script to break only if it evaluates true.

See also

More information on the Firebug script debugger can be found at `http://getfirebug.com/wiki/index.php/Script_Panel`.

Viewing the members of an ARRAY using three different methods

When the contents of a **smaller array** get confusing, alert messages may do the trick. If creating an element in the DOM to hold the output suits the project, that method is quick and easy, too. Finally, most advanced developers log this kind of output to the console, which is viewable, for one, from within Firefox's Firebug console panel.

Wrap the function in `Window.addEvent('load'),function() { ... }` so that it fires after the page completely loads.

How to do it...

Create a small array for testing. Then loop over it. Three methods are shown; only one is needed for troubleshooting. Choose one that suits personal taste and the project. For instance, a live site will only be able to accommodate the console logging method, but for a quick introspective, alert may suffice since it takes the least effort to use.

```
var my_array = ['one',2,'Trinity'];
window.addEvent('load',function() {
  my_array.each(function(array_el,index) {
    // using alert
    alert(index+': '+array_el);
    // using a text div
```

```
$('canvas').set('html',
    $('canvas').get('html')+'<br/>'+index+': '+array_el);
// using the console
console.log(index+': '+array_el);
    });
});
```

There's more...

Alerts use a modal dialogue box, which means they must be cleared before further interaction with the page. With a large array, this can cause the need for a long session of pressing the 'OK' button.

 Firefox 4 has introduced a new concept in modal dialogues for repetitive alert boxes. It includes a checkbox to prevent further alerts during the same page view. Now *that* is handy. Let's take back the Web!

Sometimes in development, it is handy to keep a floating or statically positioned DIV somewhere on the page, perhaps the bottom right. Writing a line to dump data into it is nearly as fast as alerting, but much less intrusive. Some clients reviewing development have been annoyed by alert messages.

The choice of most developers is to log information to the console. Open Firefox's Firebug console panel as seen behind the alert in this screen capture:

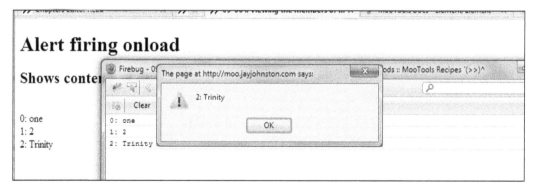

See also

Handling these same procedures with an Object is slightly different. `Array.each` is fired directly chained via dot concatenation to the instance of an array, `my_array.each(...)`. An object iterator takes a small tweak in syntax. See the next recipe for how to do it.

Viewing the members of an OBJECT using three different methods

The contents of an `OBJECT` differ from those of an `ARRAY`. Unlike an array, the keys are not incrementing integers. The values in an object have keys that may be strings or integers or even functions.

Getting ready

Create an object like a hash over which to iterate. Though objects may contain functions, only create string and integer elements for this recipe.

```
var my_object = {
    'one':'one',
    'two':2,
    3:'Trinity'
};
```

How to do it...

The iteration of an `OBJECT` varies from that of an `ARRAY` in two ways. The first is that the `Object.each()` class method must be used to begin the iteration, as opposed to iterating using dot concatenation syntax directly as is possible with an `ARRAY`. Secondly, the bound function does not return the index parameter. It does return a copy of the object.

```
Object.each(

    // 1st param is the object
    my_object,

    // 2nd param is the function to iterate with
    function(obj_val,obj_key,obj_object) {
      // the third param is the object itself
      // using alert
      alert(obj_key+':'+obj_val);
      // using a text div
      $('canvas').set('html',$('canvas').get('html')+'<br/>'+obj_
key+':'+obj_val);
      // using the console
      console.log(obj_key+':'+obj_val);
    }
);
```

How it works...

The first and second parameters are looped over by MooTools, like this `for (var key in object) {...`, where `object` in this case is the first param `my_object`. The second parameter is then used to call a function on each element.

There's more...

Returning the index may not be of much assistance, as a second `for (var key in object) {...` would be necessary to return any value derived from an index; still, to create an index, place a counter outside the iterating loop and increment within.

See also

The complete code snippet for this recipe, included with the book, shows how to affect the index incrementer.

Using the console debugger in Firefox's Firebug

The previous two recipes have already demonstrated the syntax for logging messages to a console.

```
console.log('hello world');
```

In this recipe, get ready to use the console for stepping through an application while watching the variable stack.

How to do it...

Right-click the line number and type an expression, just like you would within the parentheses of an `if` statement. In the code snippet for this recipe, on line 30, use `obj_key == "key3"`.

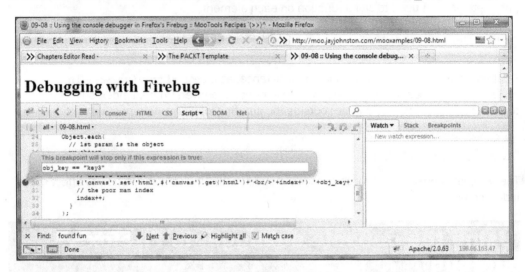

How it works...

Once the page is reloaded, the loop iterating over the object will run. On each pass through line 30, the conditional breakpoint will be evaluated. If it evaluates to true, the script is paused until the play button, or one of the other *step* controls is pressed. The play/continue button is indicated in this image by a black arrow. The second black arrow is pointing to the **Watch** window where a smorgasbord of the current variable and stack information is at our *mousetips*.

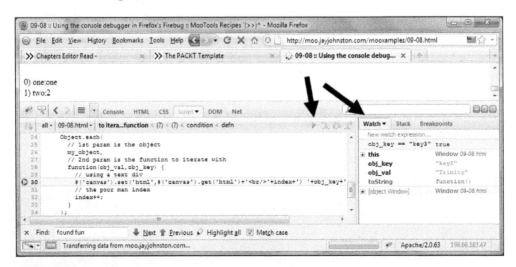

There's more...

After a breakpoint is triggered, use the *step* controls to watch the script jump in and out of the MooTools library, and all other places the code calls take the flow of the scripting design.

See also

The horror of how IE or even Safari handles some things makes us wish that Firebug was always available. Firebug Lite is an excellent option for these tough times `http://getfirebug.com/firebuglite`.

Showing an alert if an Ajax call fails

If our visitor's Internet connection fails, our script should tell them the Ajax will not work either.

How to do it...

Create a test script that makes an Ajax call. Ensure the call will fail by using a fake domain that will not resolve.

```
<form action="" method="get">
   <input type="button" id="mybutton" value="Ajax!"/>
</form>

<script type="text/javascript">
var myJax = new Request({
  url: 'http://incorrectdomain.com/nofileexists',
  onFailure: function() {
    alert('error connecting, Ajax call has failed :(');
  },
  onSuccess: function(response) {
    alert('Success! Here is the response:  '+response);
  }
});
$('mybutton').addEvent('click', function ajax_it() {

  myJax.send();

});
</script>
```

How it works...

Using a fake URL will create the same failure as a lack of Internet connectivity. The call cannot complete because it cannot contact the requested file for processing.

There's more...

If this script looks familiar, it is because it is nearly identical to the Ajax example used in Chapter 1. Of course, we have added the `onFailure` binding, but of greater importance, we are now using **unobtrusive JavaScript** to bind the click event to the Ajax function. *Chapter 1, Oldies-but-Goodies: Foundational Moo* used the `onclick` attribute of the `INPUT` button. Reduce the markup required while exercising best practices by following this unobtrusive pattern for binding events.

10
Enough Is Never Enough: Extending MooTools

MooTools, an extensible JavaScript library, begins with a base Class and then **Implements** and **Extends** classes into useful and reusable objects.

Implement the recipes in this chapter to extend what MooTools can do for you:

- ▶ Working directly with the base class, **Class**
- ▶ Extending and implementing MooTools classes
- ▶ Extending and implementing MooTools elements

Making a Corvette out of a car—extending the base class

The "base class" is a function, a method, that allows extension. Just what does extending a class entail? Buckle up and let us take a drive.

Getting ready

Just to show the output of our work, create a DIV that will be our canvas.

```
<div id="mycanvas"></div>
```

How to do it...

Creating a class from the base class is as rudimentary as this: `var Car = new Class();`.
That is not very instructive, so at the least, we add the constructor method to call at the time
of instantiation: `initialize`.

```
<script type="text/javascript">
  var Car = new Class({
    initialize: function(owner) {
      this.owner = owner;
    }
  });
```

 The constructor method takes the form of a property named `initialize`
and must be a function; however, it does not have to be the first property
declared in the class.

How it works...

So far in our recipe, we have created an instance of the base class and assigned it to the
variable `Car`. We like things to be sporty, of course. Let's mutate the Car into a Corvette
using `Extends` and passing it the name of the `Class` to make a copy of and extend into
a new class.

```
var Corvette = new Class({
    Extends: Car,
    mfg: 'Chevrolet',
    model: 'Corvette',
    setColor: function(color) {
      this.color = color;
    }
});
```

Our Corvette is ready for purchase. An instantiation of the extended class will provide some
new owner happiness for 5 years or 50,000 miles, whichever comes first. Make the author's
red, please.

```
var little_red = new Corvette('Jay Johnston');
  little_red.setColor('red');
  $('mycanvas').set('text',little_red.owner+"'s little
    "+little_red.color+' '+little_red.model+' made by
    '+little_red.mfg);
  </script>
```

There's more...

This entire example will work identically if `Corvette` **Implements** rather than **Extends** `Car`.

Whether to Extend or to Implement

Extending a class changes the prototype, creating a copy in which the `this.parent` property allows for the overridden parent class method to be referenced within the extended class's current method.

To derive a mutation that takes class properties from multiple classes, we use `Implements`.

Be sure to place the `Extends` or `Implements` property first before all other methods and properties. And if both extending and implementing, the `Implements` property follows the `Extends` property.

See also

See how Moo can muster so much class:
http://mootools.net/docs/core/Class/Class#Class.

Giving a Corvette a supercharger— Implements versus Extends

Be ready to watch for several things in this recipe. Firstly, note how the extended corvette methods can use `this.parent`. Secondly, note how the implemented corvette, the ZR1, can implement multiple classes.

Getting ready

Create a canvas to display some output.

```
<h1>Speed Indexes:</h1>
<div id="mycanvas"></div>
```

How to do it...

Here we create a class to represent a car. This car does not have an engine until it goes through further steps of manufacturing, so if we ask what its speed is, the output is zero. Next, we create a class to represent a sporty engine, which has an arbitrary speed index of 10.

```
// create two classes from the base Class
  var Car = new Class({
    showSpeed: function() { return 0; }
  });
  var SportyEngine = new Class({
    speed: 10
  });
```

Now we get to work. First, we begin by manufacturing corvettes, a process which is the extension of `Car`, they are faster than an empty chassis, of course, so we have them report their speed as an index rating one more than the parent class.

```
// Extend one, Implement the other
  var Corvette = new Class({
    Extends: Car,
    showSpeed: function() {
      // this.parent calls the overridden class
      return this.parent()+1;
    }
  });
```

Secondly, we implement both `Car` and `SportyEngine` *simultaneously* as ZR1. We cannot use `this.parent` so we return the speed if asked. Of course, the ZR1 would not have a speed if only a mutation of `Car`, but since it is also a mutation of `SportyEngine` it has the speed index of that class.

```
var ZR1 = new Class({
    // multiple classes may be implemented
    Implements: [Car, SportyEngine], // yep
    showSpeed: function() {
      // this.parent is not available
      //return this.parent()+1; // nope
      return this.speed;
    }
  });
```

How it works...

When an instantiation of Corvette is created and its showSpeed() method called, it reports the speed of the parent class, Car, adding 1 to it. This is thanks to the magic **Extends** provides via this.parent().

```
var corvette = new Corvette();
  var zr1 = new ZR1();

  $('mycanvas').set('html',
    '<table>'+
      '<tr><th>Corvette:</th>'+
      '<td>'+corvette.showSpeed()+'</td></tr>'+
      '<tr><th>ZR1:</th>'+
      '<td>'+zr1.showSpeed()+'</td></tr>'+
    '</table>');
```

And so, the output of this would be:

Corvette: 1

ZR1: 10

An instantiation of ZR1 has the properties of all classes passed to **Implements**. When showSpeed() is called, the value conjured by this.speed comes from the property defined within SportyEngine.

Upgrading some Corvettes—Extends versus Implements

Now that we have reviewed some of the reasons to extend versus implement, we are ready to examine more closely how inheritance within **Extends** can be useful in our scripting.

Getting ready

Create a display area for the output of our manufacturing plant.

```
<h1>Speeds Before</h1>
<div id="before"></div>

<h1>Speeds After</h1>
<div id="after"></div>
```

How to do it...

Create two classes, one that represents all car chassis with no engine and one that represents a fast engine that can be ordered as an upgrade. This section is identical to the last recipe; if necessary, review once more before continuing as the jist will be to alter our instantiations to display how inheritance patterns affect them.

```
// create two classes from the base Class
  var Car = new Class({
    showSpeed: function() { return 0; }
  });
  var SportyEngine = new Class({
    speed: 10
  });

  // Extend one, Implement the other
  var Corvette = new Class({
    Extends: Car,
    speed: 1,
    showSpeed: function() {
      // this.parent calls the overridden class
      return this.parent()+1;
    }
  });
  var ZR1 = new Class({
    // multiple classes may be implemented
    Implements: [Car, SportyEngine], // yep
    showSpeed: function() {
      // this.parent is not available
      //return this.parent()+1; // nope
      return this.speed;
    }
  });
```

Note that the output *before* mutation is identical to the end of the previous recipe.

```
  var corvette = new Corvette();
  var zr1 = new ZR1();

  $('before').set('html',
    '<table>'+
      '<tr><th>Corvette:</th>'+
      '<td>'+corvette.showSpeed()+'</td></tr>'+
      '<tr><th>ZR1</th>'+
      '<td>'+zr1.showSpeed()+'</td></tr>'+
    '</table>');
```

Here is what happens when the manufacturing plant decides to start putting engines in the base car chassis. That gives them a speed, where they did not have one previously. Mutate the base class by having it return an index of five rather than zero.

```
// the mfg changes base Car speed to be +5 faster
Car = Car.implement({
  showSpeed: function() {
    return 5;
  }
});

// but SportyEngine doesn't use the parent method
$('after').set('html',
  '<table>'+
    '<tr><th>New Corvette:</th>'+
    '<td>'+corvette.showSpeed()+'</td></tr>'+
    '<tr><th>New ZR1</th>'+
    '<td>'+zr1.showSpeed()+'</td></tr>'+
  '</table>');
```

How it works...

The `zr1` instantiation did not mutate. The `corvette` instantiation did. Since `zr1` used implements, there is no inheritance that lets it call the parent method.

In our example, this makes perfect sense. The base chassis comes with an engine rated with a speed of five. The `ZR1` model, during manufacturing/instantiation is given a completely different engine/a completely different property, so any change/recall of the original chassis would not be applicable to that model.

For the naysayer, the next recipe shows how to effect a manufacturer recall that will alter all Corvettes, even the ZR1s.

There's more...

There is an interesting syntax used to mutate the new version of `Car`, `Class.implement()`. That same syntax is not available to extend elements.

See also

Here is a link to the MooTool documentation for `Class.implement()`: `http://mootools. net/docs/core/Class/Class#Class:implement`.

Upgrading all Corvettes via recall— Implement AND Extend in unison!

But wait, we can do even more with `Implements` and `Extends`! Prepare to see them used simultaneously.

Getting ready

Starting off from where our last recipe left off will get us ready.

```
<h1>Speeds Before</h1>
  <div id="before"></div>
  <h1>Speeds After</h1>
  <div id="after"></div>

  // create two classes from the base Class
  var Car = new Class({
    showSpeed: function() { return 0; }
  });
  var SportyEngine = new Class({
    speed: 10,
    showSpeed: function() { return this.speed; }
  });

  // Extend one, Implement the other
  var Corvette = new Class({
    Extends: Car,
    speed: 1,
    showSpeed: function() {
      // this.parent calls the overridden class
      return this.parent()+1;
    }
  });
```

How to do it...

In this example, we want to not only speed up the 'vettes that have the base chassis, but also the ones with the sportier engine. To do this we must implement `SportyEngine` while extending `Car`, so that the speed can still cascade up from that base class.

```
var ZR1 = new Class({
    // multiple classes may be implemented
    //Implements: [Car, SportyEngine], // nope
    Extends: Car, // yep
    Implements: SportyEngine, // yep
    showSpeed: function() {
      // this.parent is not available
      //return this.parent()+1; // nope
      return this.speed+1;
    }
});

var corvette = new Corvette();
var zr1 = new ZR1();

$('before').set('html',
  '<table><tr><th>Corvette:</th>'+
  '<td>'+corvette.showSpeed()+'</td></tr>'+
  '<tr><th>ZR1</th><td>'+zr1.showSpeed()+'</td></tr>'+
  '</table>');
```

How it works...

Much like a manufacturer recall, the effort to improve the product is contingent upon the user bringing their vehicle in to receive the service. Implement into `Car` a method that provides the upgrade in speed, and then upgrade both of our mutated `Car` instances.

```
// the mfg now recalls *all* cars to be +5 faster
Car = Car.implement({
  upGrade: function() { this.speed+=5; },
  showSpeed: function() { return 5; }
});
corvette.upGrade();
zr1.upGrade();
```

And after the upgrade occurs, both the sportier engine, and the base corvette are an index of five faster than previously.

```
$('after').set('html',
    '<table>'+
        '<tr><th>New Corvette:</th>'+
        '<td>'+corvette.showSpeed()+'</td></tr>'+
        '<tr><th>New ZR1</th>'+
        '<td>'+zr1.showSpeed()+'</td></tr>'+
    '</table>');
```

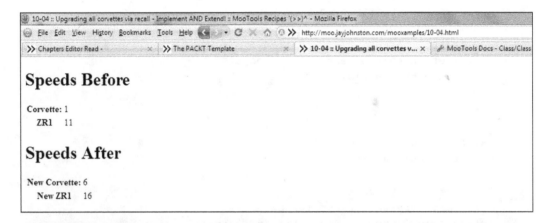

Sending a Corvette on a list of errands—extending a class with a chain

To gain some familiarity with how chains work, look in *Chapter 7, Knock And the Door Will Open: Events and Listeners* for more chaining recipes that do not include the minor complexity of **Implements**.

Getting ready

Create a canvas where the tasks completed can be written and a trigger to fire each task.

```
<h1>Taskinator:</h1>
  <form action="" method="get">
    <input type="button" value="Do Next Task!" id="taskinator"/>
  </form>
  <h1>Items Done:</h1>
  <div id="itemsdone"></div>
```

How to do it...

1. Implement the chain

2. Load the chain with actions

3. Fire off the actions in the chain

Follow these steps:

1. Create a class that implements **Chain** with a method that will append a new action to the class's internal chain:

```
var Corvette = new Class({
    Implements: Chain,
    addTask: function(task) {
      this.chain(function(){
          $('itemsdone').set('html',$('itemsdone').
            get('html')+'<br/>'+task);
          if (this.$chain.length<1) $('taskinator').fade('out');
      });
    }
});
```

2. After creating an instantiation of the class, send an array of tasks to the chain to load up the action list that our trigger will fire:

```
var little_red = new Corvette();
  // create a list of todo's to put in the chain
  Array.each([
    'drive to work',
    'drive to lunch',
    'drive back to work',
    'drive home',
    'drive to church',
    'drive back home',
    'sleep in the garage'
  ], function(el) {
    little_red.addTask(el);
  });
```

3. The trigger is fired by `Element.addEvent()`, which listens for the `onClick` event and subsequently runs `little_red.callChain()`:

```
// create a trigger to execute each task
  $('taskinator').addEvent('click',function() {
    little_red.callChain();
  });
```

How it works...

An internal set of actions is stored in an array-like format within the internal storage mechanism `$chain`. We can use the raw length of that storage mechanism to determine how many actions remain.

There's more...

MooTools **Element** has a method, `Element.appendText()`, that will allow us to append text to the top or bottom of an element node, or before or after the element node. What we need here is `appendHTML`, but that does not exist yet. Could we extend MooTools Element Class to handle that for us?

```
var Element = Element.implement({
    appendHTML: function(html) {
      var existing_html = this.get('html');
      this.set('html',existing_html+html);
    }
});
```

Ha ha! MooTools, makes it easy! Now our code is even more legible.

```
var Corvette = new Class({
   Implements: Chain,
   addTask: function(task) {
     this.chain(function(){
         $('itemsdone').appendHTML('<br/>'+task);
         if (this.$chain.length<1) $('taskinator').fade('out');
     });
   }
});
```

Extending elements—preventing multiple form submissions

Imagine a scenario where click-happy visitors may undo normalcy by double-clicking the submit button, or perhaps an otherwise normal albeit impatient user might click it a second time. Submit buttons frequently need to be disabled or removed using client-side code for just such a reason.

Users that double-click everything

It is not entirely known where double-clicking users originated from. Some believe that single-clicking-users needed to be able to double-click to survive in the wild. They therefore began to grow gills and double-click links, buttons, and menu items. Others maintain that there was a sudden, large explosion in the vapors of nothingness that resulted in hordes of users that could not fathom the ability of a link, button, or menu item that could be opened with just a single click. Either way, they are out there, and they mostly use Internet Explorer and are quickly identifiable by how they type valid URLs into search bars and then swear the desired website is no longer on the Inter-nets.

How to do it...

Extending elements uses the same syntax as extending classes. Add a method that can be called when appropriate. Our example, the following code, could be used in a library that is associated with every page so that no submit button could ever again be clicked twice, at least, without first removing the attribute that has it disabled:

```
Element.implement({
  better_submit_buttons: function() {
    if (
        this.get('tag')=='input' &&
        this.getProperty('type')=='submit') {

      this.addEvent('click', function(e) {
        this.set({
          'disabled':'disabled',
          'value':'Form Submitted!'
        });
      });
    }
  }
});
window.addEvent('load',function() {
  $$('input[type=submit]').better_submit_buttons();
});
```

How it works...

The MooTools class `Element` extends DOM elements referenced by the single-dollar selector, the double-dollars selector, and the `document.id` selector. In the `onLoad` event, `$$('input[type=submit]').submit_only_once();` all `INPUT` elements that have a `type` equal to `submit` are extended with the `Element` class methods and properties.

Of course, before that infusion of Moo-goodness takes place, we have already implemented a new method that prevents those elements from being clicked twice by adding the property that disables the element.

There's more...

In our example, we disable the submit button permanently and return false upon submission. The only way to get the submit button live again is to click the **Try again** button that calls the page again. Note that reloading the page via refresh in some browsers may not clear the `disabled` attribute; however, calling the page again from the URL or by clicking a link will.

On pages that submit a form to a second page for processing, the semi-permanently disabled button is desirable outright. If our form is processed via Ajax, then we can use the Ajax status events to manually remove the disabled property and reset the value of the button.

See also

Read the document on the MooTools `Request` class that shows the various statuses that could be used in conjunction with this extended element: `http://mootools.net/docs/core/Request/Request`.

Additionally, *Chapter 5, Mr. Clean Uses Ajax: Remote Asynchronous Calls*, has several recipes that show how to manage the state of a request using these events.

Extending elements—prompt for confirmation on submit

Launching off the last extension, the forms on our site may also need to ask for confirmation. It is not unthinkable that a slip of the carriage return could accidentally submit a form before a user is ready. It certainly happens to all of us occasionally and perhaps to some of us regularly.

How to do it...

Mutate the HTML DOM FORM elements to act upon the `onSubmit` event and prompt whether to continue with the submission.

```
Element.implement({
  polite_forms: function() {
    if (this.get('tag')=='form') {
      this.addEvent('submit',function(e) {
        if(!confirm('Okay to submit form?')) {
          e.stop();
        }
      });
    }
  }
});
```

How it works...

The `polite_forms()` method is added to all HTML DOM elements, but the execution is restricted to elements whose tag is *form*, `if (this.get('tag')=='form') {...}`. The `onSubmit` event of the form is bound to a function that prompts users via the raw JavaScript `confirm()` dialogue that either returns true for a positive response or false otherwise. If false, then we prevent the event from continuing by calling the MooTools-implemented `Event.stop()`.

There's more...

In order to mix the submit button enhancement with the polite form enhancement only a few small changes to the syntax are necessary. To stop our submit button from showing **in process...** if the form submission is canceled by the polite form request, we create a proprietary *reset* event that can be called via `Element.fireEvent()` and chained to the collection of INPUT children that match our double-dollar selector.

```
// extend all elements with the method polite forms
Element.implement({
  better_submit_buttons: function() {
    if (this.get('tag')=='input'&&this.getProperty('type')=='submit')
{
      this.addEvents({
        'click':function(e) {
          this.set({'disabled':'disabled','value':'in process...'});
        },
        'reset':function() {
```

```
                   this.set({'disabled':false,'value':'Submit!'});
                }
             });
          }
       },
    polite_forms: function() {
       if (this.get('tag')=='form') {
          this.addEvent('submit',function(e) {
             if(!confirm('Okay to submit form?')) {
                e.stop();
                this.getChildren('input[type=submit]').fireEvent('reset');
             }
          });
       }
    }
 });
 // enhance the forms
 window.addEvent('load',function() {
    $$('input[type=submit]').better_submit_buttons();
    $$('form').polite_forms();
 });
```

Extending typeOf, fixing undefined var testing

In *Chapter 9, WTFudge Is Going On?: Troubleshooting MooTools*, a discussion of variable type reporting led us to an instance where we could not properly return the type of an undeclared variable. This oddity has its roots in the fact that undefined, undeclared variables cannot be dereferenced during a function call.

In short, undeclared variables can not be used as arguments to a function.

Getting ready

Get ready to see how we can still extend MooTools' typeOf function by passing a missing variable using the global scope:

```
// will throw a ReferenceError
myfunction(oops_var);
// will not throw a ReferenceError
myfunction(window.oops_var);
```

How to do it...

Extend the `typeOf` function with a new method and call that rather than the parent method.

```
// it is possible to extend functions with new methods
typeOf.extend('defined',function(item) {
  if (typeof(item)=='undefined') return 'undefined';
  else return typeOf(item);
});

//var oops_var; // commented out "on purpose"
function report_typeOf(ismoo) {
  if (ismoo==0) {
    document.write('oops_var1 is: '+typeof(oops_var)+'<br/>');
  } else {
    // concat parent to avoid error from derefrencing an
       undeclared var
    document.write('oops_var2 is: '+typeOf.defined(
      window.oops_var)+'<br/>');
  }
}
```

The output from calling `typeof()` and `typeOf.defined()` is identical for an undefined, undeclared variable passed via the global scope to avoid a reference error.

```
<h2>without moo:</h2>
  <script type="text/javascript">
    report_typeOf(0);
  </script>

  <h2><strong>with</strong> moo:</h2>

  <script type="text/javascript">
    report_typeOf(1);
  </script>
```

The output is:

without moo:
oops_var1 is: undefined

with moo:
oops_var2 is: undefined

How it works...

The prototype for the `typeOf` function object has been extended with a new method. The original method is still applied when the function is executed. However, we are now able to call the property *defined*, which is itself a function that can still reference and call the original function.

There's more...

For those that are not satisfied at the new turn of syntax, the *proxy pattern* should suffice to help keep us using a much similar syntax.

```javascript
// proxying in raw javascript is cleaner in this case
var oldTypeOf = typeOf;
var typeOf = function(item) {
  if (typeof(item)=='undefined') return 'undefined';
  else return oldTypeOf(item);
};
```

The old `typeOf` function has been renamed using the proxy pattern but is still available. Meanwhile, all calls to `typeOf` are now handled by the new version.

See also

► The Proxy Pattern

The proxy pattern is one of many JavaScript design patterns. Here is one good link to follow for more information: `http://www.summasolutions.net/blogposts/design-patterns-javascript-part-1`.

► Undeclared and Undefined Variables

It can be quite daunting to have to deal with multiple layers of development. When we are unable to work alone and be sure all our variables are declared properly, testing every one can really cause code bloat. Certainly, the best practice is to always declare variables. Read more about it at `http://javascriptweblog.wordpress.com/2010/08/16/understanding-undefined-and-preventing-referenceerrors/`.

Extending images—add captions based on ALT attributes

Often we have to work with images, changing how we display metadata related to the images.

Getting ready

Get ready to extend images on our pages by beginning with a base class to mutate downstream classes.

```
var imgmootater = new Class({
    initialize: function() {
      this.imgs = $$('img');
    },
    make_titles: function() {
      this.imgs.each(function(el){
        el.set('title',el.get('alt'));
      });
    }
  });
```

To prevent this from being just a boring interface with no real station in life, add a common function, which is to duplicate the `IMG` tag required `ALT` attribute into the `TITLE` attribute so that mouseover actions will display the otherwise hidden metadata.

How to do it...

Extend this class while maintaining inheritance from the parent object; use the **Implements** keyword. The `initialize` function of the parent class is executed before the construct method of the new, extended object, thereby populating `this.imgs`.

```
var imgcaptions = new Class({
    Implements: imgmootater,
    initialize: function() {
```

At this point, we may now diverge from the original class. We have taken advantage of the functionality the original class designer had access to and are ready to move on. Still, that bit about adding the title text was pretty good.

```
      this.make_titles();
```

There, now we can go on with our new functionality. Wrap each image in a DIV that has the image itself, a break, and the metadata from the ALT tag.

```
this.imgs.each(function(el) {

        // handle the excessive margins of the imgs
        var margin = el.getStyle('margin');
        el.setStyle('margin',0);

        // wrap the img, set styles, insert caption
        var c = new Element('div');
        c.inject(el,'before').grab(el).setStyles({
           'margin':margin, 'text-align':'center'
        }).set('html',c.get('html')+'<br/>'+el.get('alt'));
     });
   }
 });
```

How it works...

Now that we have a base class to make titles, we can instantiate that as follows.

```
//usage for imgmootater:
   var cpt = new imgmootater();
   cpt.make_titles();
```

The cool thing about inheritance, is that we took that first guy's class object and implemented it into our own. To have that functionality *AND* our own, we need only instantiate our own, newly extended class object instead. That might look like this.

```
   new imgcaptions();
```

Because we put all our functionality for the `imgcaptions` object within the construct, there is no need to call a function on the instantiation. It does all the work required, including that which `imgmootater` would do if we called `make_titles()`.

There's more...

The next recipe shows how yet a third developer might reuse `imgmootater` for his or her purposes.

Extending images—lazy load

Here again, we extend our base object `imgmootater`.

Getting ready

And, again, the preparation for this recipe is the `imgmootater` class itself. Sound the trumpets!

```
var imgmootater = new Class({
    initialize: function() { this.imgs = $$('img'); },
    make_titles: function() {
      this.imgs.each(function(el){
        el.set('title',el.get('alt'));
      });
    }
});
```

How to do it...

Extend the `imgmootater` class. Perhaps somewhat academically, we are extending something that already does an action we need. In this case, at least academically, we are demonstrating a recipe that shows that `imgmootater` does a great deal of important, reusable work. In this example, what it does is duplicate the ALT attribute metadata into the TITLE attribute so that mouse over shows the metadata.

The new implementation of the class will be called `lazyloader` and will focus on IMG elements that have a place-holding image as their SRC. Add an `onScroll` event to the window and bind to it the class function, which checks to load all images that have now been scrolled *above the fold*.

Above the Fold

This terminology is said to have been brought about by the newsprint industry. Any items that were found on the newspaper without unfolding the paper or turning it over were "above the fold". This made much more sense in that industry given that all news papers were folded identically. Web browsers and monitors play a variable role in where exactly the "fold" will appear at any given time. We are gentle with clients that request that things show up "above the fold" while also recognizing that if our script must load images "above the fold" then we must dynamically determine just quite where it is for each individual user.

```
var boundload;
    var lazyloader = new Class({
        Implements: imgmootater,
        initialize: function(spacer) {
            this.make_titles();
            this.spacer = spacer;
            // we need to bind "this" to this.loadimgs
            boundload = this.loadimgs.bind(this);
            // now we can pass the bound function to addEvent
            window.addEvent('scroll',boundload);
            window.addEvent('load',boundload);
        },
        loadimgs: function() {
            // always redefine which elements to loop over
            this.imgs = $$('img[src='+this.spacer+']');
            // stop eternal calling to this method once complete
            if (this.imgs.length==0)
                window.removeEvent('scroll',boundload);
            // what is the viewable area?
            var wscor = window.getCoordinates();
            var wspos = window.getScroll();
            // stop any browser loading of imgs below fold
            this.imgs.each(function(el){
                var pos = el.getPosition();
                if (pos.y<=wscor.bottom+wspos.y) {
                    el.set('src',el.get('longdesc'));
                    el.removeProperty('longdesc');
                }
            });
        }
    });
```

How it works...

▶ Instantiate the Extended Object

We will not require the return value of instantiation. Simply use the **new** keyword, and be sure to pass the path to the spacer image, which is acting as a place holder.

```
new lazyloader('10_spacer.gif');
```

▶ Determine the Fold

The "fold", as it were, is determined by using the MooTool Core included `window.getCoordinates()` and adding it to the current scroll of the page `window.getScroll()`. Any element can use these two methods, not just the window.

▸ Determine IMG position

One other method of `Element.Dimensions` is `getPosition()`. Once the IMG element in question has a y position less than the window's scrolled position, the actual image source hidden in the XHTML valid `LONGDESC` attribute is switched into the SRC attribute and the image loads.

▸ Save browser memory

To prevent the script from continually checking to load images, once all images have been loaded, the `boundload` method of `lazyloader` is removed from the `onScroll` event of our window.

There's more...

Say, what happened to the nifty extended class that put captions on our images? For the purposes of trying to keep the recipe short, the intermediary class and its captioning functionality were left out. Have no fear, though, the code snippets in the book include a version that implements *both* classes to demonstrate MooTools' superior inheritance properties.

```
var lazyloader = new Class({
    Implements: [imgmootater,imgcaptions],
...
```

Here is a screen capture showing how `imgmootater` is duplicating the metadata attributes, `imgcaptioner` is placing the IMG tags in captioned DIVs, and `lazyloader` is only loading the IMGs that are above the (current) fold.

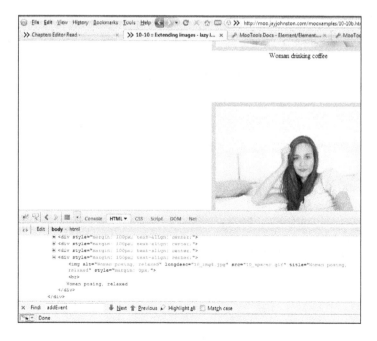

See also

Follow up on the documentation for `Element.Dimensions` in the MooTools documentation: `http://mootools.net/docs/core/Element/Element.Dimensions`.

Loading Google fonts!

The world is a-buzz with the excitement of every designer on the planet. Finally, we can use something other than Arial, Helvetica, and Verdana!

Get ready

Produce some markup that we can use to apply our Google fonting to.

```
<h1 style="font-family:'Miltonian'">Hello, my fine world</h1>
  <h2 style="font-family:'UnifrakturMaguntia'">World, you are
    fine indeed</h2>
```

 The styling using `font-family` does not have to be inline. Using it within the stylesheet is perfectly acceptable. All information in Google's documentation for the font library stands; our extended class will only abstract and simplify the loading of the fonts.

How to do it...

The embed code for Google Fonts is pretty straightforward. Still, in an effort to make it simple even for non-technical designers, reduce the instantiation to a mere:

```
new GWFLoader({fontcsv: 'Miltonian,UnifrakturMaguntia' });
```

In order to pass the options and deep set them, extend the **Options** class in MooTools. That way we can pass in the comma-separated list of fonts that we wish to load from Google's library.

```
var GWFLoader = new Class({
    Implements: Options,
    options: { fontcsv: '' },
    initialize: function(options) {
      this.setOptions(options);
```

The next step to take while still in the constructor is to explode the CSV of fonts and validate them. A free, JSON service that returns a list of valid fonts exists at `http://jayjohnston.com/google_font_directory.php`.

```
this.fonts = this.options.fontcsv.split(',');
    new Element('script',{ src: 'http://jayjohnston.com/
        google_font_directory.php?callback=GWFLoadingBinding&x='
        +GWFInstance, type: 'text/javascript' }).
        inject(document.head);
    eval('GWFLoaderBinding'+GWFInstance+' = function(gwfdir) {
        this.set_fonts(gwfdir); }.bind(this);');
    GWFInstance++;
},
```

When that Ajax request returns, call several internal methods, in turn, which finally embed the requested fonts.

```
set_fonts: function(gwfdir) {
    this.gwfdirfonts = gwfdir.fonts;
    if (this.fonts[0]!='') this.validate_fonts();
},
validate_fonts: function() {
    // check to be sure the font requested exists in the
        google library
    this.fonts.each(function(font){
        font = font.clean().replace(/ /g,'+');
        if (!(this.gwfdirfonts).contains(font)) {
            this.fonts.erase(font);
            alert('font '+unescape(font)+' is not in the google
                library');
        }
    },this);
    this.embed_fonts();
},
embed_fonts: function() {
    var family = 'family=';
    this.fonts.each(function(font,i) {
        family += escape(font.clean());
        if (i<this.fonts.length-1) family += '|';
    },this);
    new Element('link',{ rel: 'stylesheet', type: 'text/css',
        href: 'http://fonts.googleapis.com/css?'+family }).
            inject(document.head);
    }
});
```

How it works...

Google fonts itself returns, based on browser type, an embedded font file, which the browser then parses to fulfill the styles request for a given font-family.

Take a look at the beauty of embedded web fonts. NOTE: These *are not* images; they are text!

There's more...

The next recipe shows how to dynamically load a multi-select box that shows all the available font-families and dynamically builds the instantiation code. How much easier can it get?

See also

More and more fonts are being loaded all the time:
http://code.google.com/apis/webfonts/.

Extending the Google Font Loader

In the recipe we just looked at, we extended the Options class, took an option in the form of a CSV of Google fonts, and styled text using CSS. Get ready to see how even the instantiation line can be generated based on a few clicks. That way, no typos or issues with unavailable fonts can creep in and catch us off guard.

Designers, especially, love this one-time-use class method.

How to do it...

Dabble in a bit of polymorphism. When no fonts are passed during instantiation, route the flow of action to a new method that generates an interface. That interface will have a multi-select input widget that onClick updates a TEXTAREA with an instantiation code that designers can use to embed their Google web fonts.

For brevity, only the new method is shown:

```
    ...
    generate_code: function() {
        // for each of the styles  available, create an li
        // display in multiselect format, generate code on click
        this.fonts = [];
        this.gwfdirfonts.each(function(font) {
            this.fonts.include(font); },this);
        this.embed_fonts();
        new Element('select',{
            multiple:'multiple',
            size:'10',
            style:'width:500px;font-size:20px;line-height:20px;',
            id:'gwfpicker'
        }).inject(document.body,'bottom');
        new Element('textarea',{id:'gwfcode',style:'height:500px;
            width:400px;vertical-align:top;'}).
            inject('gwfpicker','after');
        this.fonts.each(function(font) {
            new Element('option',{
                text: font.replace(/[+]/g,' '),
                style:'font-family:''+font.replace(/[+]/g,' ')+'''
            }).inject('gwfpicker','bottom');
        });
        $('gwfpicker').addEvent('change',function() {
            var fonts = '';
            var ops = this.getChildren('option');
            ops.each(function(op,i) { if (op.selected)
                fonts += op.get('text').replace(/ /g,'+')+',';
            }); // replace space w/ +
        var js = 'new GWFLoader({fontcsv:';
        js += "'"+fonts.substr(0,fonts.length-1)+"'";
        js += '});';
            $('gwfcode').set('html',js);
        });
    }
});
```

How it works...

Two new elements are created. The first is a multi-select, which contains one SELECT OPTION for each of the currently available Google web fonts returned by the free JSON service. For additional user friendliness, each option is further styled by a background embedding of *every Google web font*. Be sure to give it a few seconds to load.

Instantiation of the Google web font picker is the same as loading fonts with the class; just do not send any argument, and the option to generate the desired instantiation is presented. Click while holding the control key (*Ctrl*) to select multiple fonts.

```
// instantiation *without any options*
// routes flow to GWFLoader::generate_code();

    new GWFLoader(); // handled by GWFLoader::generate_code();
```

The Google web font loader font picker (yay)...

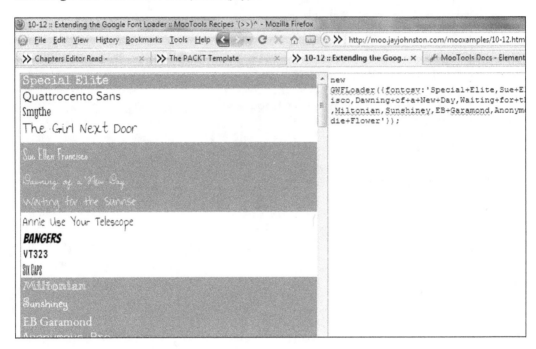

There's more

This example attempts to comprise just about every technique used throughout the book within a single recipe. There is more, more, more of this in much smaller, bite-size doses throughout the book. Be sure to look though other chapters as well.

Index

T

table
  injecting, into HTML DOM 67, 68
tall page
  displaying 87, 88
TD data cell
  injecting, into TR table row 63, 64
template object 20
test() method 44
TEXTAREA element 188
toBottom() 87
Toggle() method 96
toInt() method 44
transitions
  image movement, animating 201-203
TR data row
  injecting, into table 65, 66
trim() method 44

troubleshooting, MooTools. *See* **MooTools, troubleshooting**
tween() method 93
typeOf
  extending 240-242

U

uniqueID() method 44
User Interface (UI) 85

W

web service
  displaying 124-126
  parsing 124-125
window widgets
  dragging, on screen 156-158
  location, recording with Ajax calls 162, 163
  switching places 159, 161

Thank you for buying
MooTools 1.3 Cookbook

About Packt Publishing

Packt, pronounced 'packed', published its first book "*Mastering phpMyAdmin for Effective MySQL Management*" in April 2004 and subsequently continued to specialize in publishing highly focused books on specific technologies and solutions.

Our books and publications share the experiences of your fellow IT professionals in adapting and customizing today's systems, applications, and frameworks. Our solution based books give you the knowledge and power to customize the software and technologies you're using to get the job done. Packt books are more specific and less general than the IT books you have seen in the past. Our unique business model allows us to bring you more focused information, giving you more of what you need to know, and less of what you don't.

Packt is a modern, yet unique publishing company, which focuses on producing quality, cutting-edge books for communities of developers, administrators, and newbies alike. For more information, please visit our website: www.packtpub.com.

About Packt Open Source

In 2010, Packt launched two new brands, Packt Open Source and Packt Enterprise, in order to continue its focus on specialization. This book is part of the Packt Open Source brand, home to books published on software built around Open Source licences, and offering information to anybody from advanced developers to budding web designers. The Open Source brand also runs Packt's Open Source Royalty Scheme, by which Packt gives a royalty to each Open Source project about whose software a book is sold.

Writing for Packt

We welcome all inquiries from people who are interested in authoring. Book proposals should be sent to author@packtpub.com. If your book idea is still at an early stage and you would like to discuss it first before writing a formal book proposal, contact us; one of our commissioning editors will get in touch with you.

We're not just looking for published authors; if you have strong technical skills but no writing experience, our experienced editors can help you develop a writing career, or simply get some additional reward for your expertise.

Google App Engine Java and GWT Application Development

ISBN: 978-1-849690-44-7   Paperback: 480 pages

Build powerful, scalable, and interactive web applications in the cloud

1. Comprehensive coverage of building scalable, modular, and maintainable applications with GWT and GAE using Ja

2. Leverage the Google App Engine services and enhance your app functionality and performance

3. Integrate your application with Google Accounts, Facebook, and Twitter

4. Safely deploy, monitor, and maintain your GAE applications

NetBeans IDE 7 Cookbook

ISBN: 978-1-849512-50-3   Paperback: 308 pages

Over 70 highly focused practical recipes to maximize your output with NetBeans

1. Covers the full spectrum of features offered by the NetBeans IDE

2. Discover ready-to-implement solutions for developing desktop and web applications

3. Learn how to deploy, debug, and test your software using NetBeans IDE

4. Another title in Packt's Cookbook series giving clear, real-world solutions to common practical problems

Please check **www.PacktPub.com** for information on our titles

Joomla! 1.5 JavaScript jQuery

ISBN: 978-1-849512-04-6   Paperback: 292 pages

Enhance your Joomla! Sites with the power of jQuery extensions, plugins, and more

1. Build impressive Joomla! Sites with JavaScript and jQuery

2. Create your own Joomla!, jQuery-powered, extensionsn

3. Enhance your site with third-party features, code-highlighting, Flicker, and more using Joomla! Plugins

4. Detailed explanations with step-by-step guidance and practical examples

MooTools 1.2 Beginner's Guide

ISBN: 978-1-847194-58-9   Paperback: 280 pages

Learn how to create dynamic, interactive, and responsive cross-browser web applications using this popular JavaScript framework

1. Learn how to build super-charged web forms

2. Learn how to write powerful and flexible cross-browser code

3. Make your web applications more dynamic and user-interactive with AJAX

4. Packed with examples that will show you step by step the most important aspects of getting started with MooTools

Please check **www.PacktPub.com** for information on our titles

www.ingramcontent.com/pod-product-compliance
Lightning Source LLC
Chambersburg PA
CBHW080359060326
40689CB00019B/4065